WHY ENTREPRENEURS REALLY FAIL

Why Entrepreneurs Really Fail

The Road to Success ...
Always Under Construction

Nozer Buchia

BLOOMSBURY
LONDON • NEW DELHI • NEW YORK • SYDNEY

Bloomsbury Publishing India Pvt Ltd
Vishrut Building, DDA Complex
Building No. 3, Pocket C-6 & 7, Vasant Kunj
New Delhi 110 070

ISBN: 978-93-82951-60-5
10 9 8 7 6 5 4 3 2 1

Typeset by Eleven Arts
Printed and bound in India by Replika Press Pvt. Ltd.

CONTENTS

FOREWORD

This book is written by an experienced International Entrepreneur.

Nozer has juxtapositioned failure and success in Entrepreneurship and shown how people-oriented the road to success can be. The book contains his rich personal experiences and insightful observations.

This book would be a worthwhile read even if it was limited only to his personal experiences; however, he has made it even more valuable by adding his advice and direction for changing failure into success.

The "seven habits for winning" could be a valuable book by itself, as the author uses his years of experience to guide you from losing habits to winning behavior.

The author places great emphasis on partnerships or partner-like relationships.

He points out the importance of balancing these relationships and using them for all the positive purposes that partnerships make possible.

On the other hand he points out that the Entrepreneur's position is not a team sport, and that the Entrepreneur must take ultimate responsibility for leading the enterprise.

Not many books emphasize failure as a method of succeeding.

When you have finished reading this book you will understand how failures can be a method of building strength for the future.

I cannot think of any person, whether one considering entering the field of Entrepreneurship, or one experienced in business or as an Entrepreneur, who would not prosper by reading this book.

William W. Sherrill
Former Governor—Federal Reserve

Founder/Chairman Emeritus
Wolff Center for Entrepreneurship
Bauer College of Business, University of Houston
Houston, Texas, U.S.A.

Entrepreneurialism is typically something that is part of one's DNA, and not a skill that can be taught.

To the first-time skater, it looks easy watching an Olympic Gold Medal Winner perform.

But one must experience the countless trips and falls on the ice before one can perform successfully.

In short, you must pay your dues before you achieve greatness.

In ***Why Entrepreneurs Really Fail***, Nozer Buchia is successful at providing those "lessons learned" to help accelerate the entrepreneurial process, so that you can achieve greatness much quicker.

Remember … winning is a habit … and so is losing.

David G. Wallace
Sugar Land, Texas, U.S.A., Mayor 2002–2008

I have known and worked with Nozer for several years.

We share a passion and curiosity about what drives Entrepreneurs and how to build Organizations.

Nozer is a rare original thinker who can motivate people to think and behave differently.

His experiences, both good and bad, as a businessman are both interesting and educational.

His willingness to share his defeats as well as his victories as a way to trigger learning is a sign of true servant Leadership.

Bill Boyar
Chairman, Boyar Miller
Attorneys-at-Law
Houston, Texas, U.S.A.

Entrepreneurship in the modern world has become a part of our everyday life. We all aspire to grow beyond our day-to-day survival, and seek to learn how the other person has does it. Well, we have to wait no more, for in this book **WHY ENTREPRENEURS REALLY FAIL... *The Road to Success Always Under Construction***, Nozer Buchia has so aptly described WHAT TO DO to be successful by highlighting WHAT NOT TO DO in order to avoid failure. I find this book to be extremely motivational and an excellent thought provoking guide for successful life and business strategies.

I have been associated with Nozer since the early 1980's and have always found him to be a person that does not rest till he finds a solution to a problem or an issue that has confronted him. I distinctly remember a legal matter on which we had worked together along with the iconic Mr. Nani Palkhivala, where Nozer portrayed his never-give-up-attitude and displayed his entrepreneurial skills by compelling the team to think out-of-the-box and collectively resolve the issue at hand. I recollect his pet phrase that has always lingered in my mind for all these years – "there is always a way, we just have to find it; just because we cannot find it does not mean it does not exist... it only means that we are not trying hard enough and are therefore not yet ready to succeed."

It is indeed rare to find people with the qualities that Nozer Buchia possesses. He is a born entrepreneur. The one thing that I have always admired most about Nozer is his willingness to help others succeed, by guiding them and not allowing them to make the same mistakes that he has had to struggle with in his life and in the world of business. His effortless pursuit of entrepreneurship and his desire to allow people to grow by compelling them to get out of their comfort zone is extremely admirable, to say the least.

Also lovingly referred to as 'Mr. Motivator', Nozer is a great speaker, an excellent coach, and above all a 'growth-artist' that transforms non-performing and under-performing people and organizations, and moves them towards the path to success. He mesmerizes audiences with his infectious humor and real life experiences, for he speaks with great conviction, and during his 36 years in business, he has lived what he talks about.

I feel privileged to have been associated with Nozer for all these years, and to be able to contribute my thoughts on this book, which I believe is a must read for all those that have the desire to do something great in life. I wish Nozer the best in life always!

Mr. Homa Petit
Partner, Vigil Juris
Advocate & Solicitor
Mumbai, India

PREFACE

The book you are holding is the result of countless mistakes and umpteen errors that I have committed in life and in the world of business.

Each time that I thought I had finally mastered the recipe for success, something unexpected happened; something that I had not thought of, something that I had never planned. And once again, success eluded me!

I would get that burst of energy repeatedly, to try that one more time, but then it all went back to status quo. I was scared.

I desperately wanted to succeed, but was very afraid that I might fail...... again. What if I was not destined to be an Entrepreneur? What would people say? What would they think of me?

I started doubting my potential, my capability and my ability to get the job done. I started analyzing my chances of success before I had even begun.

But then I realized and experienced the fact that success and failure are merely a frame of mind. If you think you are beaten; you are. You need to believe in yourself if you want to achieve anything in life.

This gap between success and failure provoked this book.

While this book is about mistakes and failures, it is also about how to be a winner. It draws on my years of experience as an Entrepreneur and the various lessons that I learned along the way.

The pages of this book will demystify for you, why some people always succeed while others merely just fail. You will understand how negative habits can be disastrous to your success and how failure can be used to turn things around.

This book will demonstrate to you that the Entrepreneur normally stands alone in this wicked world of business, and if not careful, can fail with an irrecoverable chance for success.

I have drawn a ton of inspiration from people along the way that have taught me to be more humble than I actually thought I was. I have learned that to be on the right track, one must first have a defined track to be on.

The ultimate lesson that I learnt is very clear; believe very passionately in the things that you do, and success will soon follow.

This book is not just for dilettantes, nor even just for the intellectually curious. It is not even written just for the Entrepreneur that is simply beginning.

It is a handbook for those that want to lead and are not merely content to follow. It is for people that want to make a difference. It is for the ones that are passionate to succeed. It is a path for those that want to rewrite the rules of the game and are not afraid to challenge the way it has always been done.

'*Why Entrepreneurs Really Fail*', is the missing link between your yearning for success and your attainment of success.

Nozer Buchia

ACKNOWLEDGEMENTS

A Big Thank You

The best classroom
In the world
Is at the feet
Of a wise person

My Parents...Departed but not forgotten

To my dear departed parents, my mom, Coomi Buchia and my dad, Jemi Buchia; who have taught me all the values of life, thank you so much for having me.

You have been the best parents any child could possibly have. As you have both always engrained in me, and I quote, "the biggest and best gift parents can give their children is the ability to think on their own". This gift that you let me 'earn' has been the best thing you have done for me in my life.

You refrained from picking me up before my fall, but were ready and waiting, to guide me as how not to fall again. You anticipated my mistakes, but never rushed to correct me, as you wanted me to be stronger by way of self learning and through my own experiences. Your actions and support, gave me the strength I needed to continue, in spite of my errors and mistakes, and for this I will be eternally grateful.

You helped me put my feet on the ground, by putting responsibility on my shoulders. I learnt from you that it is not what you do for your children, but what you have taught them to do for themselves, that will make them successful.

Thank you for allowing me to learn through my failures, knowing that you were always beside me to help and support me when I needed it most. I know you are watching over me and guiding me from above. I pray that your souls rest in everlasting peace.

My Mentor

To my mentor and guide, Noshir Dubash; thanks for taking the time to be my friend. Your words of wisdom are the gems that I think of everyday, and wish I had the good sense to believe in them earlier then I actually did.

Never let emotions
Get in the way
Of a business decision

I am reminded of your expression that has left a lasting impression on my mind, and I quote, "The only thing that stands between a man and what he wants from life, is often merely the 'will' to try it, and the 'faith' to believe that it is possible".

Your ability to solve problems amazed and intrigued me for many years, till I finally understood how you did it; you just never gave up! You were not afraid to share your knowledge with me and you absolutely convinced me that everything in life is within ones reach. It is up to each one of us to grab it, the very first time, and make it ours.

Your motivation and your commitment to my success, has enriched my world of Entrepreneurship in a way that one cannot even imagine. You have positively influenced my life and my career and have allowed me to grow and prosper as an individual.

May you attain eternal salvation.

Family Really Matters

My Offspring

To my children Shiraz, Aarish and Kyrus; you are truly a gift from God, a gift that I will always love and cherish. In spite of all the mistakes that I have committed in life, you have taught me to be a much better person, more tolerant, more understanding, more loving and most importantly a student all my life.

The questions that you have asked me have challenged my mind and made me think and be prepared with answers, just so that I could be one step ahead of your next question. You have encouraged me to get rid of behavior that does not add any value to one's self or for that matter one's family.

In your own way, you have educated me to accept the fact that the greatest natural resource is the minds of our children. An ideal parent is one that is willing to learn from the wisdom of their children. You have

Get rid of behavior
That does not add any value
To your success

taught me that children need to be treated as co-pilots of a plane rather than passengers in a train.

To my other son, Kermaan Irani—thank you for helping me realize and understand that relationships are vital and very important, and need to be nurtured and cared for, even if you did not give birth to them.

My Better half…

And finally to my better half, the love of my life, my wife Persis; thank you for walking with me all through life. I would never have made it this far without you by my side.

It is so wisely said, that if you get a good life partner you are *complete,* else you are *finished.* A spouse can either make a person or break a person.

You have certainly stood the Entrepreneurial test of time, for when I almost wanted to give up and walk away, you held my hand tight, and pushed me again and again to get up and try, just that one more time.

You have sharpened my thinking, and have convinced me to accept the fact that to get out of difficulty, one must usually go through it.

Your precious words of encouragement meant more to me than anything in this world; "You will make it this time… I believe in you"!

Life teaches you through people

Life has taught me that nothing great has ever been achieved without taking calculated risks. I learned that one must do what is difficult or untried, for the surest way to learn is through our own mistakes and the mistakes of others.

Gold medals don't make champions, hard work does. And so does attitude to believe and to belong.

*Life sometimes gives you
a second chance...*

*It is up to you to grab it with both hands,
say thank you and do something with it*

To those of you that could not do much for me in life (at least that is what my egotistical and ignorant self thought at the time), I say thank you; for you have taught me a vital lesson of life; one should keep his words soft and tender, because tomorrow he may have to eat them.

To those of you that made me feel derisory and extremely inadequate when you were in power, I say thank you; for it was only your arrogance and unwarranted behavior that helped me become more determined to succeed.

And to all those people that have influenced my thinking, I say thank you, for from each and every one of you I erudite something; from some of you I learned what to do and from some I learned what not to do.

CHAPTER 1

Are You Ready

The temptation to quit
Will be greatest
Just before
You are about to Succeed

Have You Started Yet

If you have already ventured out on your own then what I write in this book is for you. If you are struggling with an idea and do not know what to do next, then this book is for you. If you are stuck and growth is eluding you, then also this book is for you.

It will enable you to identify your strengths and acknowledge your unique capabilities. It will assist you to more clearly understand what you need to do, to be immensely successful in the world of business. It will also open your eyes to what not to do, and minimize your risk of failures.

Remember, a person is successful because he does not let failures stop him. He continues onward, learning from his past and improving his future. He moves ahead with an unreasonable power to make things happen.

The Unreasonable man

As George Bernard Shaw has said, and I quote, "The reasonable man adapts himself to the world. The unreasonable one persists in trying to adapt the world to himself. Therefore all progress depends on the unreasonable man".

It is those awkward moments in life when we feel so lonely and so desperate that all we want is to give up. That is exactly the time when we need to chug along, keep going, never give up, but instead work smarter and find new ways to accomplish our dreams.

Learn from My Mistakes

And through this book, and my various interviews and speaking engagements, I am committed to guiding those that want to plunge into the world of Entrepreneurship.

*Self confidence is the first
prerequisite to success*

I learned things the hard way in life and want to make it a little easier for those after me. I say to the skeptics and non-believers that the difference between failure and success is in your heart and mind.

What I have learned has not come simply from books but from the school of hard-knocks in life. I am not ashamed to state that I have failed several times but have not quit. I have made bad judgment calls many times in my career and have even taken incorrect decisions.

I have learned through my mistakes, for I believe that in life as in business, one must have the freedom to make mistakes, as that education is the surest way to really experience true success.

My Entrepreneurial journey started with a simple belief. The belief that I could be successful if I tried hard enough and never gave up; even when times were tough and the whole world seemed against me.

There were times (and believe me there were ample occasions), when I felt so hopeless that I regretted even venturing down this path of establishing myself as an Entrepreneur.

I felt so alone and clueless that sometimes I would even wonder if I knew what I was doing. It seemed like the right thing to do; but how does one continue when one does not know what to do next.

And all those people that you believed would support you, for you had helped and stood by them at some point in their lives, slowly moved away, giving one excuse or another. They did not want to be associated with a person that was struggling to make it in business and therefore in life—they were more worried and concerned about their social status in the world.

And that is when I concluded that there comes a point in your life when you realize who matters, who never did, who won't anymore and who always will.

During times like these I always ask myself one question—what is the

Take charge of your destiny

worst that can happen. And the answer I get—nothing so damaging, which cannot be managed.

And that gives me the courage to get up and continue, to forge ahead as if nothing really had stopped me in the first place.

My quest for business and Entrepreneurial salvation has been very slippery and challenging to say the least, but very educational and extremely rewarding.

And I share this with you, not to be cherished or admired, but to enable my experiences to serve as a source of guidance, support, direction and encouragement for you in your quest for business deliverance.

There are many ways to business and personal success in this book. I encourage you to discover them and adapt them in your pursuit of business excellence.

CHAPTER 2

My Entrepreneurial Journey

Failure...
Is the surest way to Success

My Mentor—My Guide

Decades ago a very wise and learned man once told me "Each one for himself, God for all and devil take the hindmost. Never be last in this race" he said. "Remember you are in business to make money; so trust no one in your quest for business salvation till you are absolutely certain about their motives. Life is very transactional in the business world and people will want you for what you can do for them, at the moment you can do it. After that you will become history!"

This man was Noshir Dubash, my mentor, my friend, my guide. I always thought he was too pessimistic, extremely unrealistic at times and non-business-like, even though I knew in my heart, that he was ahead of his time. But his advice always lingered at the back of my head for I knew that he genuinely cared for me and wanted me to be successful in life and in the world of business.

And had I paid heed to his advice, I would have avoided all those pitfalls and anguishes that I faced in life, for as a businessman then, I would have thought first from the head and then from the heart.

I would have saved more money than I spent and learned more lessons than I taught. I would have accepted that failure is the surest way to success and that friendship has hardly any place in business. I would have learned sooner, that Entrepreneurs must always reinvent themselves as learners, as learning is central to their survival and hence to their growth.

And today, decades later, I want to tell him that he was right; but I can't—he has attained his salvation and is now in a better place. He knows he is being missed.

My Rock—My Mom

Realization soon dawned on me that life does not go to the bigger or stronger man but goes to the man who thinks and believes he can. For every stone that someone threw at me, I used it to build my castle;

You never lose when you fail
You lose only when you quit

the structure on which I finally built my dreams, my aspirations and my values.

Each time someone whispered "This is so very difficult you will not be able to do it...don't even try it", my stubborn but confident self would say, "Watch me carefully, I will do it".

And for this I am indebted to my mom, Coomi Buchia, for she instilled this in my head, "there is always a way son you just have to look for it. Just because you cannot find it does not mean it doesn't exist. If you want to succeed in the world you must make your own opportunities". She ingrained in my head that self confidence is the first prerequisite to success, a statement that I have always carried with me all my life.

She was my rock, a rock that I looked up to each time and wondered "How does she do it?" And before I realized the answer my rock left me for her heavenly abode, left me when I needed her the most. May her soul always rest in eternal happiness.

I quickly learned that the toughest part of getting to the top of the ladder is getting though the crowd at the bottom. For I would find people ready to persuade me as to why something could not be done. And they even sounded very convincing at the time.

But by then life had taught me that to be successful it is more important to reach the people that count than to count the people you reach.

My Dad—*My Hero*

As my dad, Jemi Buchia often told me, "Son, a successful person never loses because he never quits". My dad never quit. He always made things happen. I was always fascinated by his will power and his ability and tenacity to go from one success in life to another. I loved him immensely but respected him even more for what he had achieved in his career and his life.

He always told me "take charge of your destiny... learn to put your

Success is the Ability
To go from
One Failure Another
Without any loss of Enthusiasm

shoulder to the wheel and things will happen. If you develop a burning desire to be successful, trust me son, you finally will".

The tenacity and resolve with which he kept going on and on in life, left me wondering whether this was what all Entrepreneurs actually did to be successful. But then I had read about unsuccessful people too, which compelled me to believe that what my dad did was something really exceptional.

One day my curiosity got the better of me and I finally asked him what it all meant and how he did it. "What is the secret of your success dad?" I asked.

And he gave me that loving smile, a big Daddy-Hug and that million dollar answer that I will never ever forget. "Success", he said, "is the ability to go from one failure to another without any loss of enthusiasm. Only those that understand and accept failure can master and achieve success".

How I wish he was with me today, to guide me with his thoughts and motivate me with his words. But he is now in a better place and guiding me from above; I am certain.

Experience—A Comb Life Hands You When You Go Bald

As I sail along the road of life, Einstein's words run through my mind and keep reminding me to never give up, for as he said "successful people have always encountered violent opposition from mediocre minds".

Success keeps you glowing, but only persistence keeps you going. The key to success is to continue learning throughout your life with a voracious appetite, for from some people you learn what to do, from others you learn what not to do.

Ability
Talent
Motivation
Attitude
Results

With all positive and prolific influences in my life, my faith has been strengthened, my emotions are now contained and my thinking has greatly matured.

I have come to accept, that before we endeavor to take our primary steps to being successful, it is very important, first, to know ourselves and our abilities.

We have to be true to our inner self for then and only then, can we step out into this unforgiving world of Entrepreneurship, and make a difference. Only those that recognize and acknowledge their weaknesses can be prepared to use their strengths and their abilities for their ultimate betterment.

Do we really *know* ourselves?

I mean do we know our tendencies and patterns? Do we know how we learn and how our mind thinks? It is called self awareness. It is very vital to know yourself well, and can become a valuable asset to understand how you lead and where you might fail as a Leader. Most of us really don't understand ourselves as deeply as we should. I am speaking from experience.

The more I work to become a better Leader the more problem areas arise, and I see patterns that need more work. I think of myself as a good communicator but at times fall short of understand the patterns of others and therefore over-communicate or under-communicate in specific situations. My ability to communicate therefore needs to be adapted to specific circumstances.

There is usually a large disconnect between who you think you are and what you are actually perceived to be. Being conscientious is very different from being competent. Most of us confuse the two and believe that they are interchangeable. That is not the case at all.

So, do we really know our capabilities, our abilities and our value? Do we acknowledge out limitations at any time? We are so self-absorbed

A man
Who has to be convinced
To act before he does
Is not man of action

that realization does not dawn until it is really too late. The key to self realization is self assessment. Ability, motivation and attitude are the natural ingredients that are much needed for ones success.

And there is only one proof of ability—results! And results can only be achieved through action. I would, any day, prefer chaotic action to orderly inaction, for honors and rewards fall only to those that show their good qualities in action.

In my opinion, it is not enough to 'will', one has to 'act'. Remember, a sleeping lobster is carried away by the water current.

If you want to succeed *TALK* about yourself

In advancing through life one also has to realize that one does not get fame or recognition just because one thinks he deserves it; someone else has to think so, too. Learn to gain access to the people on top, for until they know you, they can't help you.

I quickly learned that advertising is the mouthpiece of all businesses. If you want to be noticed, whenever you do a thing, act as if the whole world is watching.

As Bill Boyar, Chairman of Boyar Miller, an excellent attorney and a great strategist and businessman once told me, "all press is good, as long as they spell your name right".

Talk about yourself with pride and people will accept you. Talk about what you can do for them and they will be compelled to listen to you. Talk about how they would benefit from their interaction with you and they will be your spokesperson for life.

Kodak sells film but they don't advertise film. They advertise memories.

I was once asked at a seminar as to what I thought the most perfect product in the world would be—and my immediate answer—'the best

JOB...
Just Obey the Boss

product in the world will have German engineering, Japanese quality and American marketing'.

I have embraced the fact that American marketing is probably the very best in the world, for it has taught me two distinct things... stand up to be seen and speak up to be heard.

Actions Speak *Louder* Than Words

So get started. Learn to strike when the iron is hot. In fact, not only strike when the iron is hot, but make it hot by striking; for our strengths often increase in proportion to the obstacles that are imposed upon us each step of the way.

In the long run we only hit what we aim at, so why not aim at something high. And if we miss, let us try again.

Business is like riding a bicycle—either you keep moving or else you fall down. And if you do fall down get up and ride again. Stop complaining. As a wise man once said, "Quit crying over spilt milk; instead go milk another cow". Or as Dale Carnegie would state, "When fate hands you a lemon, let's try and make lemonade".

Or better still, "when life hands you lemons, ask for Tequila and Salt and call me over".

In my experience, there are three different types of people in today's world of business—those that make things happen, those that watch things happen and those that wonder "What happened?"

I often ask myself this question, where has that burning desire to start something new in life, vanished. Why are people so content with mediocrity? Why do we take the easy road and get a job (JOB after all spells... **J**ust **O**bey the **B**oss) versus trying to start a business venture. Of course there are several reasons for this, the most important one, I believe, being guidance.

Destiny is not
A matter of chance
It is a matter choice;
It is not a thing be waited for
It is a thing be achieved

Williams Jennings Bryan

I have come across many individuals that have all the right ingredients for starting out as an Entrepreneur, they just do not know what to do or how to get started.

Does Luck have a role in Success

Having acknowledged what Williams Jennings Bryan has said, personal experiences have taught me that 'luck' still plays a big role in life and in business.

The great Thomas Jefferson has said, "The harder I work, the luckier I get". True. Hard work is an essential ingredient in the pot of success, but luck certainly plays a very vital role.

I have seen talented people never make it to the top. On the other hand, I have witnessed average individuals with constrained or sometimes even no talent be very successful, because, as they say, 'all their heavenly stars were aligned'. They were at the right place at the right time.

Believe me, for I have personally experienced this in my life and my Entrepreneurial career. It is indeed very frustrating, to say the least, but very true.

Luck permits you to be at the right place at the right time, so as to grab that opportunity of a lifetime.

Luck certainly has a big part to play in success, but not big enough for us to sit on our haunches and simply hope for things to happen. We have to keep striving for success.

Luck favors those that help themselves.

CHAPTER 3

Entrepreneurship... the Road to Success

Winners are too busy
To be sad,

Too positive
To be doubtful,

Too optimistic
To be fearful

And too determined
To be defeated

Entrepreneurship... Expect the Unexpected

With a wealth of knowledge gained through personal experiences and failures in life and in the world of business, it is my firm belief that Entrepreneurship is the key to success. When a person has the gift of Entrepreneurship, nothing can stop him.

In my opinion the world belongs to the Entrepreneur.

So how does one define an Entrepreneur? How does one define success? And how does one measure it?

In the words of Ronald Regan, "American Entrepreneurs are the men and women of faith, intellect, and daring who take great risks to invest in and invent our future".

My definition of an Entrepreneur is an individual that has the courage to suffer personal and business losses whilst pursuing a business venture. An Entrepreneur isn't an Entrepreneur until he has met a payroll— trust me on this one! Sounds simple doesn't it? Let us evaluate what it really means.

Courage & Intuition... are they for real or is it a myth

Courage, in my opinion, is not the absence of fear but the strength to do what is right in the face of it. And believe me, most of us have far more courage than we ever dreamed we possessed.

If you lack the courage to start, you are then already finished. Winners win because they have the courage and the burning desire to win. If you don't have the courage, BUILD IT, else don't get started.

Personal and business losses are inevitable on the road to success. Some of you might argue—why personal losses. Because they are unavoidable and will certainly occur as you pursue your quest for Entrepreneurship. Start by accepting this fact.

To get something
You never had
You have to something
You never did

Your business venture will be a third-party in your marriage or relationship with your significant other, and will be a big burden on your sense of togetherness.

Low energy—mental, emotional and physical; little or no vacation, unsteady income, missed holiday dinners, a 24/7 work schedule, balancing the home and business, will all cause you to develop a sense of uncertainty and anxiety, and will lead you to doubt your biggest asset—your capability.

The Entrepreneurial road is very slippery and quite unknown as you never know what you might face and when you might experience it. You will feel confused, bewildered and even scared to decide on which path to turn into when you reach that dreaded fork in the road.

Both ways will seem so real and achievable and it will be impossible to ascertain, at that very moment, the correctness of your decision.

In times like this, I have relied on my gut-feel, my intuition, and it has seldom let me down. Believe me this is so true... I have personally experienced it!

Gut Feel & Intuition—A lesson from my four-legged friend

Talking of gut-feel and insight, I learned a vital lesson from our family dog, Oliver. He is a beagle with a nose that can smell a drop of pee in a gallon of water.

Each morning when I take him out for his morning walks, he religiously does two things—every time; leads me all the way during his walk (his trainer, Malcolm, will have a fit after reading this), and has his nose to the ground, making way and preparing his next move. I really did not pay any attention to this daily routine, till one day I realized why he actually did it.

Intuition and persistence
Will get you
Where you need to be

His leading the way was sending a message to me that he was in control, not me. If I insisted on leading the way, he would let me, but only for a short time. After that he was back to his normal self, back in control, well ahead of me.

Guess what—after a few times of trying, and thanks to my Blackberry, I gave up (his trainer, Malcolm, will have a seizure now, I think) and let him lead me to where he wanted to go. Victory through persistence!

And talking of the blackberry, don't you think the world was a much relaxed place when APPLE and BLACKBERRY were just fruits... just a thought!

Oliver's nose to the ground is the surest way for him to follow his instincts—his gut-feel. He goes berserk when he smells something in the ground. And each time he does that I think about why he succeeds. His instincts tell him what is ahead of him so he can plan his next encounter. And as soon as he accomplishes his task, he wags his tail, telling the world, I am happy I followed my gut. Sweet smell of success!

And talking of dogs, do you know why a dog has more friends than a man—it is because he wags his tail more than his mouth. He boasts of success only after he has experienced it!

The Entrepreneurial Trap

In my opinion two types of Entrepreneurs aren't worth a dime—those that never do what they are told and those that do nothing else except what they are told.

- So what is the trap into which Entrepreneurs often fall?
- Is it lack of foresight
- Is it that they do not go with their intuition
- Do they chase their dreams with no definite plan for success
- Is it that they spend too much time planning and then fail as they lack the skill and ability to execute?

The will to succeed is
The first condition of success...
For success measured by the
Willingness keep trying

- Is it money
- Or is it something else

I think the trap they fall in depends on the reasons they started down this path in the first place.

Let us then define the critical issues that need to be understood before we can proceed to identify the obstacles to success for an Entrepreneur. Let us also define the reasons that corrupt an Entrepreneur's behavior and thereby jeopardize chances of success. Let us also define success and how to measure it.

Obstacles to Success

In the words of Winston Churchill; a man that gave his people strong Leadership and great devotion that ultimately led to Britain's military salvation—"Success is not final, failure is not fatal: it is the courage to continue that counts".

So I say to you here and now, when you reach the end of your rope, tie a knot in it and continue to hang on, success will soon follow. Keep your eyes on the stars and your feet firmly on the ground, and success will soon follow. Just because fate does not deal you the right cards, does not mean you should give up. It only means that you should play the cards you have to their maximum potential.

In my opinion, Ray Kroc was the first businessman to apply the principles of mass production in a service industry. He was a school drop-out but a master at creating an everlasting brand.

When Ray Kroc officially established The McDonald Corporation, he was 52 years old, had lost his gall bladder and most of his thyroid gland, and suffered from severe diabetes and arthritis. But he continued on his Entrepreneurial journey for, in his own words, "I was convinced that the best was ahead of me".

The world will expect you to accomplish something before it lets you feel good about yourself

The $2.7 million that he paid to buy all of McDonalds is considered to be one of the greatest acts of salesmanship of all time.

An Entrepreneur needs to develop a burning passion to be as optimistic as possible; for an optimist overcomes hurdles and obstacles and goes where no man has gone before—literally.

A pessimist, in my opinion, procrastinates before he decides not to take a chance.

- A pessimist sees difficulty in every opportunity whereas an optimist sees an opportunity in every difficulty; a sure way to success
- A pessimist always sees his glass half empty; an optimist always believes his glass is half full
- For a pessimist, strength comes from physical capacity; for an optimist strength comes from an indomitable will
- A pessimist is an appeaser who feeds a crocodile hoping it will never eat him; an optimist will kill the crocodile today as he knows at some point in time it will surely want to eat him

Where others see obstacles real Entrepreneurs see opportunity. And opportunity rarely knocks till you are ready. So let us highlight the hurdles that an Entrepreneur needs to be conscious off before he commences on his business venture.

Debt
Borrow as little as possible

A borrower becomes the lenders slave. No matter how you look at it, this statement is accurate—believe me, I should know!

As Benjamin Franklin once said, "I would rather go to bed without dinner than rise in debt". Debt is not bad as long as one understands the repercussions.

Get Better or get Beaten

Jack Welch

The situation that most Entrepreneurs find themselves in today is a disparity between debt and equity. It is also a classic example of "over leveraging" and then of course the age old curse, recourse v/s non-recourse debt; i.e., signing personal guarantees for the debt.

The loan-to-value ratios determine the strength of your holdings when confronted with a situation like the economic downturn in which we are today. It also helps in refinancing the debt with the existing or even a new lender.

In the end, all business operations and processes can be reduced to three simple but powerful words;

- People
- Product
- Profit

The engine that drives enterprise is not thrift, but profit. And debt, if not handled right, can be the killer of all profit. All debt is not bad; what is bad is the way it is structured, the way it is contained.

Debt improves Return on Investment (ROI) and provides the flexibility of doing business with Other People's Money (OPM); which most people believe is the only way to do business.

The key is to develop a structure in your business where you borrow what you need and only what you really need, and feel less threatened by it.

Wait Till You Have It
Don't spend before you earn

Plan your finances so well that you do not make the mistake of spending what you do not have. Planning will force you to think and be prepared for most eventualities in business.

Debt is an Obligation
Avoid it at all cost... if you can

Most first time Entrepreneurs commit the classic mistake of spending in anticipation of incoming revenues and expected profits. It is like spending monies that you do not have, at least not at that present moment anyway.

Most businesses that I have had the chance to observe, have failed simply because the Entrepreneur was presumptuous about the outcome of the business. He would spend based on anticipated earnings that never materialized. This would then lead to increased borrowings, which amplified risk and put the Entrepreneur in a vulnerable position.

This is also true about Entrepreneurs reinvesting all their earnings back into the business—a classic and stupid mistake I made several moons ago. After all, ready money is Aladdin's lamp. With money you are on top of the world. Cash is King, so learn to save it; if you have to spend it, spend it wisely.

Spend it only when you have it and only after you have saved some of it. Do not over extend yourself and for your own sake and that of your family, don't ever live a life that you cannot afford.

I call it the S.I.E.E. syndrome.

- **SAVE** as much as you can, for a dollar saved is a dollar earned. Savings will enable you to have the power you need to be confident in life and in the world of business.
- **INCOME** increase is the surest way to allow for savings, which can, in turn, create a sizeable nest-egg for the future. This will make you independent in life.
- **EXPENSE** reduction enables proper financial management, and therefore additional savings. The less you spend means the more you save.
- **EDUCATION** will assist you in increased income which in turn allows you to save more. Ask the price of education to an illiterate man.

My Principle of POP...
PLAN or PERISH

- **EXPERIENCE** is the glue that allows for a set discipline to ultimately achieve financial bliss. Experience will lead you to your ultimate goals by helping you avoid those pitfalls in life.

If you do not know how to plan your finances or are not sure about how to go about it—get advice!

Did you know that people find it easier to talk about their sex lives than their financial situation?

As Bill Gates has so often said, 'If you are born poor it is not your fault, but if you die poor, it is'.

Fear

Never give up your RIGHT to be WRONG

Fear is a feeling of concern and anxiety, a distressing emotion aroused by impending danger; whether the threat is real or perceived.

Although fear is natural, we must put it aside if we are to ever take control of our lives and live life to the fullest.

The key to success is to overcome all fear, to never hold yourself back and to push yourself to what you really want to achieve. When you face your fear, most of the time you will discover that it was not really such a big threat after all.

Fear does not have any special power unless you empower it by submitting to it. Most Entrepreneurs fear the unknown and therefore lower their goals and aspirations instantly when faced with adversity.

It is because we fear failure that we tend to shy away from making decisions unless we are sure those will ultimately enable us to be successful. We curtail our basic instincts to act and negotiate due to fear of failure.

THE S.I.E.E.E. SYNDROME

Save...
As much as you can

Income increase...
Will help savings

Expense reduction...
increase savings

Education...
Is the key to success

Experience...
Is the glue

We instantly start believing in the worst and start preparing for it, thereby unconsciously ignoring that self-confidence that we had built up for our success.

Fear takes away our ability to think. It destroys our vision, our poise, our self-assurance, and leads us into accepting the fact that we may not succeed. We may fail.

We all fear failure, but fail to understand that failure does not mean that I am a failure; it only means that I have not yet succeeded.

And what we also forget is that fear is self-imposed. It is the way we think that causes us to fear things. Therefore, to avoid 'fear' we need to start thinking differently. We need to think with confidence. We need to believe in ourselves.

I personally accept the fact that most of us have, sometime in our life, operated out of fear. We have been 'scared' to move forward due to the fear of being 'not successful'.

This conversation between a reporter and a very successful business illustrates my point accurately.

Reporter:	Sir, you have been successful in life and in business. What is the secret of your success?
Businessman:	Right Decisions
Reporter:	And Sir, how do you make right decisions?
Businessman:	Experience
Reporter:	And how do you get experience?
Businessman:	Wrong decisions

As the great Indian Leader Mahatma Gandhi once said "Freedom is not worth it if it does not include the freedom to make mistakes".

Let us learn from our children who I think are our greatest natural resource and the best Entrepreneurs of them all. They have no fear of the word NO!

Let us never negotiate
Out of fear,
But let us never fear
To negotiate

President John F. Kennedy

They forget the last transaction very quickly, however challenging it was, and are at it again, this time with even more persistence. They have NO FEAR of failure.

In my opinion there are few successful adults that were not first, successful children. If you want to be successful you have to learn to conquer fear itself!

- Fear of failure in business, curtails our ability to make decisions
- Fear of failure as a social impediment leads us to be extra cautious as we want to be perceived as always being successful
- Fear of criticism and the 'I told you so' syndrome dissuades risk taking, which is the fundamental root of Entrepreneurship.

In either case it is fear that causes a person to be extra guarded and extra conservative and therefore less effective and less successful.

My experience has led me to believe that most people never really succeed because they do not operate in an effective zone. They are instead satisfied being in their comfort zone. They find very uncomfortable, the extra effort to shift from their comfort region into their effective region.

But what we have to remember is that it is the shift, which is also called *growth*, is what will make them productive and therefore ultimately successful.

If you want a good shot at success, get out of your comfort zone, push yourself hard and learn to operate in your effective zone.

No Goal Setting
Have Consistency of Purpose

The secret to success is consistency of purpose as the most successful of us have goals and purpose.

The world will not care
About your ego
Or your esteem

To forget one's purpose is the commonest form of stupidity. A planned three-step approach to goal setting will enable an Entrepreneur develop and determine a vision for success.

- Where are we today
- Where do we want to go
- How do we get there

And in order for this to be reinforced, it must be in writing.

In baseball, great hitters keep a 'book' on every pitcher so that they know his tendencies.

- Put that goal in writing
- In business what gets measured gets done
- Your goals will enable you to stay focused at all times
- It's not about being busy, it is about results. Focus on outcomes
- Set personal and professional goals in writing
- Goals will help you achieve the balance in life that you seek. Seek it and you'll find it!

Most people 'don't' expect to be really successful and therefore 'they're' not. There's a huge difference between positive expectations and negative ones.

Concentrate on finding your goal, then focus on reaching it. The greatest thing in business is not so much where we are, but in what direction we are moving.

As one of the greatest real estate tycoons of all time, Donald Trump, has said, "I aim very high, and then I just keep pushing and pushing and pushing to get what I'm after".

A business without goals is like a body without a soul. When you lose sight of your goals, all you see is obstacles.

*Freeze the Fear
And Push the Envelope*

Remember, goals are the end towards which all efforts should be directed if one wants to achieve ultimate success. Goals provide a sense of direction and purpose.

If we are disciplined enough to set goals and then track their progress, there is not any goal in life or business, I think, that cannot be achieved.

Chasing the Business
Learn to attract it

It is similar to the laws of attraction—Chasing the business v/s learning to attract it. You need to begin working ON the business not IN the business. If you want to be a big Company tomorrow, you have to start acting like one today. It is critical to improve your effectiveness and reach by demonstrating the value of your business. For price is what one pays; value is what one gets.

Ray Kroc, founder of McDonalds, has taught the world that in order to attract business, you must create the need in another person, by convincing him to see and accept your product or service as actually being so much better for him.

As Ray has put it, "It takes a certain kind of mind to see the beauty in a hamburger bun!" It is up to the Entrepreneur to enable the creation of that mind. And most often than not, it is done by appropriately branding the product or service.

To attract business you only have to be slightly better but with a differentiating factor. And in order to differentiate you from the competition and attract business, a personal note of advice... attempt to go where no man has gone before.

In business, there are two types of mentalities, push and pull. To be successful, an Entrepreneur needs to develop the ability and the knowledge to *pull the business in.*

Whoever said...
"It's not whether
You win or lose"...
Probably lost

And a good way to attract business is to attract the right people to work in your business. No general can fight his battles alone. He must depend on his ability to secure the right man for the right place.

Lack of Knowledge
Know your employees and your customers and your business

During a surprise visit at a factory, the CEO of a manufacturing Company saw a young man leaning against the wall doing nothing. He went up to him and asked him "How much do you earn young man?" The young man answered "about a $1000 a month Sir".

The CEO asked his Financial Officer to get him $2000 in cash, gave it to the young man and said "here is two months' salary—you are fired, now get out of my factory. Around here I do not give money to people for just standing around doing nothing". The young man was in utter shock and left as fast as he possibly could.

Noticing fellow employees staring at him in disbelief, he also said "and that applies to everybody in this Company". He then turned to his Financial Officer and asked him "who was this guy I just fired?" The Financial Officer replied "He was the pizza delivery guy Sir".

As John M. Clark has so correctly stated, "Knowledge is the only instrument of production that is not subject to diminishing returns". And the essence of knowledge is not simply having it, but using it; for an investment in knowledge always pays the best interest.

It is very often said that employees are our biggest asset. I vehemently disagree. Since when on earth have employees become assets? I thought an asset was something that you owned—land, building, machinery.

Employees are not your assets they are your investors. They invest their time, energy and skill into your business and we simply look at them as a cost to the organization. We have to start thinking differently.

A Great mind
Has a set purpose
All others
Only have desires

We have to change the way we look at things that add value to us and our organization. We have to make them feel proud of being associated with the organization. A team motivated by pride is much better than a team motivated by fear of the boss.

And as far as customers go, it is them and only them that determine how big any Company should be. It is the oldest lesson in the business world; unless you are customer driven, you go out of business. IBM succeeded because it always acted as if it was on the verge of losing every customer.

Years ago, a disappointed salesman of a large Cola Company returned from his Middle East assignment. A friend asked, "Why weren't you successful with the Arabs?"

The salesman explained "When I got posted in the Middle East, I was very confident that I would make a good sales pitch as Cola was virtually unknown there.

But, I had a problem I didn't know to speak Arabic. So, I planned to convey the message through three distinct picture posters.

First poster: *A man lying in the hot desert sand... totally exhausted and fainting.*
Second poster: *The man is drinking our Cola.*
Third poster: *Our man is now totally refreshed.*

And then these posters were pasted all over the place. "Then that should have worked!" said the friend.

"You bet it should have' said the salesman, except that I didn't realize that in that part of the world, people read from right to left".

"So what they saw was a totally refreshed man, drinking our Cola and then lying in the hot desert sand—totally exhausted and fainting".

*Your goals will determine
Your thoughts...
Your thoughts will determine Your life*

Talk about lack of knowledge!

No Exit Strategy
Establish an exit criterion and monitor it

In business, real wealth is normally created when Entrepreneurs pass the reins of their business to another person, i.e., when they exit the business.

Very few Entrepreneurs have been 'lucky' enough to create wealth by being at the right place at the right time. The rest have planned for years and executed the plan to the best of their ability.

They have prepared themselves for all eventualities and have steered their companies in a direction that compels a prospective buyer to view them seriously.

The final portion of a business plan must outline an exit strategy. Your exit plan needs to be clear in your mind because it will dictate how you operate your Company.

An exit plan must have a strategy and a goal for it to be successful.

Successful Entrepreneurs plan their exits well ahead of the expected time to pass on the 'baton'. But also, let it be acknowledged that no matter how sound and robust a business strategy is, it is only as good as the result it achieves.

Exit strategies can be for long-term involvement or for short-term attachment.

An Entrepreneur may decide to close the doors of the business and liquidate remaining assets, or sell his shares to another partner or simply sell everything at market value and use the money to pay off all remaining debt.

Progress
Has little to do
With speed...
But a Lot to do
With direction

On the other hand he may decide to go public, or merge with another Company, or be acquired by another organization, or simply sell his Company outright for a quick exit.

An exit strategy is nothing but embracing change, a change in lifestyle, in behavior, in attitude and most importantly in financial stability.

And an exit strategy will only be successful if it is timed right.

Right Place at the Right Time

Timing is everything when an Entrepreneur decides to move out. Greed will cause you to wait for more. It is at that time that prudence must prevail.

Your Principles of Operation will determine your success or failure in this ever changing world of business.

As I have always said, and I repeat; have a plan and execute to that plan. If you do that successfully, the governance of your plan, will force you to perform in a manner that will be conducive to running an organization that is surely bound to succeed.

A Millionaire before the age of 25

Let us look at the lives of these six millionaires (as reported by Kiplinger staff on October 18th, 2010), that made it well before their 25th birthday and let us learn what they have to say about their success.

Mark Zuckerberg—co-founder of Facebook

Mark is a geek-to-billionaire story that has become the basis of the hit movie "The Social Network". "Young people are just smarter", he told a Stanford audience in 2007. He started Facebook from his Harvard dorm in 2004 as a sophomore. Now he's a 26-year-old

Do not fix your Weakness...
Strengthen your Strength

philanthropist, recently donating $100 million to the Newark, N.J., school district.

Zuckerberg's youthful fame and fortune, is the result of vision, smarts, determination, and a little luck.

I also believe it was his time to act, and he seized the moment.

Catherine Cook—founder myyearbook.com
Made her first million by age 18

In 2005, Catherine and her brother founded the social-networking site, which functions like a digital yearbook with pictures, friends and virtual currency called "lunch money." Today, it boasts 20 million members and is one of the 25 most-trafficked Web sites in the U.S.

Her advice for young Entrepreneurs: "Stop just thinking about it, and make it happen.

When you're young is the best time to start your own business, as you do not have the responsibilities you will have when you're older. The worst that can happen if you fail now is that you have firsthand experience to make your next venture a success."

Sean Belnick—founder bizchari.com
Made his first million by age 16

Belnick's been selling business furnishings online for nearly a decade now, but the recent B.A. graduate of Emory University's Goizueta School of Business still saw value in a college education.

His advice for young Entrepreneurs: "It is never too early to start. I started when I was 14. There was a lot of great information on the Internet. Just do the research and find a way to do what you want to do."

*Address your Employees
By their Name*

Juliette Brindak—co-founder and CEO missOandfriends.com
Made her first million by age 19

Brindak won't divulge when she earned her first million, but says that her Company was valued at $15 million when she was 19.

At 10, Brindak started drawing the "cool girls" cartoon figures who became stars in 2005 of her online community for teen girls. Today, she is seeking investors and preparing to take the site public as she attends Washington University in St. Louis.

Her advice for young Entrepreneurs: Find a solid support team who believe in your idea. "If someone starts to doubt your Company and what you're doing, you need to get rid of them."

Matt Mickiewicz—founder Sitepoint99 Designs and Flippa
Made his first million by age 22

Mickiewicz, who launched his first Company in 1998, points out that the Internet enables immediate customer feedback, making it relatively inexpensive to test and launch new ideas.

His advice for young Entrepreneurs: "People who say it takes money to make money are using the worst excuse ever ... Create massive value for others by providing a solution where no other exists."

Michael Dell—founder and CEO Dell Computers
Made his first million by age 19

Dell launched his computer Company in 1984, just before dropping out of the University of Texas. By selling direct, Dell lowered prices and won over customers. At 24, the Company had revenues of $258 million. At last check, his estimated net worth was $13.5 billion.

Turn your workers into Entrepreneurs...
Share your
Knowledge and ideas
And reward them
For doing the same

His advice for young Entrepreneurs: "You've got to be passionate about it," he said in an interview with the Academy of Achievement.

"I think people that look for great ideas to make money aren't nearly as successful as those who say, 'Okay, what do I really love to do? What am I excited about?'"

So what do we learn

Having examined the lives of successful individuals I have come to the conclusion that success comes to those that have the courage to perform and the good sense to act when the time is right.

But I also believe that luck has a role to play in an Entrepreneurs' success. Most people believe that it is all about timing and less about luck. I say the two go hand-in-hand.

Timing to me is *seizing* the moment and acting quickly. Luck is *getting* that moment to act quickly and succeeding. That is why I say that the two go together.

Successful people are always looking for ways to be successful. They have their eyes and ears open for opportunities that may otherwise elude common individuals. They do a ton of research and look for avenues that bring about success.

Then they act.

I can say this from experience that no matter how you look at successful people, there is certainly an element of luck that favors them.

But they did not just wait for luck in order to get that special treatment; what they did was to act, and the rest just fell in place.

1. It all starts with proper **Planning**. You need to be fully aware and very determined as to where you really want to go. Remember my principle of POP; Plan or Perish.

Everyone wants to be
On top of the mountain,
But all the contentment and Development
occurs when
You are actually climbing it

2. **Organizing** enables you to put that planning into action. You start by following the plan that will ultimately lead you to a path of success.

3. Remember you cannot do it all by yourself. **Staffing** is that key ingredient that will run the engines of your business. Get the right people, empower them, then sit back and watch the magic as it happens.

4. A Leader is a catalyst, he makes things happen. He removes all obstacles so others can operate in an environment that breeds success. **Leading** is enabling others to be successful.

5. **Controlling** is tracking success.

And then of course it finally depends on the governance...

    i. where are we today,

   ii. where do we want to go,

  iii. how will we get there

If I were to list a few reasons that differentiate successful Entrepreneurs from unsuccessful ones they would be as follows...

- Go with your intuition (gut-feel)
- Set goals in writing
- Overcome fear
- Know and understand your customer
- Plan or Perish (the principle of POP)
- S.I.E.E. syndrome (SAVE much, INCOME increase, EXPENSE reduction, EDUCATION certainly helps, EXPERIENCE is the glue to financial stability)
- Borrow as little as possible
- Don't spend before you earn
- Push the envelope
- Stay the course

Don't compare your Life
To that of others
You have idea what their
Journey all about

- Hire the right staff & reward them well
- Have an exit strategy

And bear in mind you Entrepreneurs out there, a simple proven rule to grow your business—Be fearful when others are greedy and be greedy when others are fearful.

In conclusion, more people have created steady wealth by being masters of their own destiny. It is much easier and extremely rewarding if you take the blame and the credit as well.

CHAPTER 4

Seven Deadly Habits

That Corrupt

An Entrepreneur

Broadcast your Strengths,

Tackle your Weaknesses,

Capitalize on Opportunities,

Minimize all Threats

Winning is a habit... unfortunately so is losing

My road to success has always been under construction for whenever I found the key to success, somebody changed the lock.

And that gets me even more resolute than ever before.

In spite of that I never gave up but instead forged ahead relentlessly, for each time that I came across a road block in my career, I remembered the words of my mom …

There is always a way son you just have to look for it. Just because you cannot find it does not mean it doesn't exist. It only means that you are not trying hard enough.

Her words constantly remind me that to be successful you only have to be 1% better; that there is nothing you cannot do in life with the right focus and a positive attitude.

Most Entrepreneurs convince themselves that rewards will start coming routinely once they have ventured into the field as Entrepreneurs and have what they call 'an identifiable position' in life.

They start business ventures for the wrong reasons and then wait for life to treat them fairly. What they cease to understand and accept is that life does not always give you what you want. Nor does it grant you what you may think you so richly deserve.

I believe that life does not always go to the bigger or the stronger man, but instead life goes to the one who believes he can (I said that earlier as well). And then, remember, to get something you never had, you have to do something you never did.

We have fixed perceptions about our strengths and weaknesses and are very quick to blame 'fate' for our condition in life. We are so inured to accept what comes our way that we sometimes keep doing the same things over and over again expecting a different result. We are victims of our way of life, our routines and our habits.

If you follow people
All you see is their back side
Lead... don't Follow

Habit # 1

We are born to win but are conditioned to fail; believe in your self

There are many reasons but no excuses. Success is when skill meets opportunity; failure is when fantasy meets reality.

I have seen so many Entrepreneurs fail and give up for one and one reason alone; they just do not know what to do when failure engulfs their business and their lives.

They have been conditioned to accept the fact that they are not destined to be in business and immediately start the process of self pity.

When successful people fail, they look at it as a mistake and move on to create more successes. The rest of us immediately start the process of 'I do not have the luck', or 'I am not destined to be in business'. If you believe you can you will, else you will not.

As my friend and a remarkable PGA Championship golfer Doug Sanders has said, and I quote, 'When a winner makes an error, he admits it; when a loser makes an error, he says, it was not my fault. A winner always tries to improve the situation; a loser says that's the way it has always been done'.

What we say to ourselves, affects our performance which in turn affects our attitude through our subconscious thinking, and causes us to get on the path of negativity.

And negativity instantly builds a case for why you cannot do something. What we always believe in our subconscious to be true is not really true.

Remember Santa Claus! You believed in him because you were made to believe it, till you gained more affirmative information that altered your thinking.

Remember...
You are not defined by your past
You are prepared by your past

In 1962, four young musicians played their first record audition for the executives of Decca Recording Company. The executives were not impressed. While turning down this group of musicians, one executive said, "We don't like your sound at all. Groups of guitars are on their way out".

The group of musicians was very disappointed. They discussed their frustration, brooded a lot, but decided to keep on playing because they believed in their talent and more importantly, themselves. The group was called The Beatles!

As Thomas Edison so aptly said "I will not say that I failed a 1000 times, I will say that I discovered there are 1000 ways that can cause failure".

Wouldn't it be nice if, when we mess up our life we could simply press 'Ctrl Alt Delete' and start all over again?

But in reality, and as my beloved wife Persis would say, "Life is not a dress rehearsal dear husband; this is the real thing; better get used to it"!

As Bud Hadfield, founder of Kwik Kopy has so eloquently said, and I quote, 'We all have the talent to fail. Some are better at it than others. But all failures are temporary until you accept one of them as permanent'.

I have come to realize that the difference in our success or failure is not change but choice. Because when adversity strikes, it's not what happens that will determine our destiny; it's how we react to what happens. How you choose to respond will determine your altitude in life—the choice is yours.

Habit # 2

Are you a Priority in people's lives or are you their Option—Which one are you?

I have often been asked the secret of success. And my response; "I do not have a silver bullet that will underscore the secret of success.

The only difference
Between stumbling blocks
And stepping stones
Is the way in which
You want to use them

However I do know the secret of failure; trying to please all the people all the time".

This certainly is one bad habit an Entrepreneur must religiously shy away from because attempting to always please will cause you to be defensive about your actions and be answerable about your behavior, to those that do not really count.

Remember no matter how successful you are in the world of business, or for that matter how many times you have failed in a business venture, our answer to people that ask questions should always be selectively categorized; because those that matter don't mind and those that mind don't matter!

There is a new term in physiatrist studies called 'relationship-illness'. Look at the people in your lives and ask yourself these four questions...

- What is this relationship really doing 'to' me
- What is this relationship doing 'for' me
- Does it put me on the winners stand or on the losers list
- Does it help my inner self develop or does it force me into a state of negativity

Trust me, some people are so negative that they would probably walk into a dark room and start developing!

Life is not waiting for the storm to pass; it's about learning to dance in the rain. And if you are being restricted by another to explore your personality, then you need to change that relationship. You need to walk away else you will be sucked into a world of gloom and despair.

The words of my mentor keep ringing in my ear ever so often; "...you must be in charge if you want to be successful in business. Be selfish (if you have to) but be in control. If you allow others to dictate how you do your business then you are finished even before you start. And always have Plan 'B' in place".

Do not worry about people
From your past;
There is a good reason
Why they did not make it
To your future

This always makes me think of BATNA—Best Alternative to a Negotiated Agreement.

In this world of business always have an alternative!

And remember there is only one person in the world that will look after you and that is you.

No one is in charge of your happiness but you. Your life is powered by you and no one else matters.

This has been one habit that has pulled me down in life and in business. I have sacrificed my time, energies, priorities and even my family, for the benefit of others that have used me to their ultimate gain and success.

But was it their fault? The answer is NO! It was my fault for allowing myself to be used.

Habit # 3
Performance v/s Position…. Our Perception

A priest and a cab driver both died and went to the pearly gates where St. Peter awaited their arrival. He looked at the priest and said "Welcome Father John.

You have been a source of inspiration to all on earth. You helped those in need, guided those in pain and served the Lord with all you heart and mind. You get the key to the silver room".

And he turned to the cab driver and said "You are Joe the cab driver. I know you very well. You drove all over New York. Well here is your key to the golden room".

Hearing this Father John gets upset, begs forgiveness and states "I served the Lord, helped those in pain, prayed every day, did everything that I was asked to do in life, performed to the best of my abilities and I get the silver

Winners feel like winners...
Losers act like losers

room. This is just Joe the cab driver and he gets the golden room. After all it was I that had a position in life".

And St. Peter replied "Father, your perception about your position in life is flawed. Your performance has been great but Joe achieved more than what he was sent on earth to achieve. His performance has been just spectacular". *"And how is that" asked Father John.*

And St. Peter replied, "Father when you prayed people slept, when he drove people prayed".

We rarely think outside the box and often let our emotions get the better of us. Most of us expect to get a high 6-digit salary as soon as we get out of business school. Our perception about our position in life and in business changes as soon as we get our business degrees.

We soon incorporate our companies, buy new business suits, print new business cards possibly with the words 'President' on it and expect to be called business people and treated fairly.

Trust me it just does not happen. Some of us start businesses and expect to be profitable from day one. This does not happen either.

I strongly believe that Business schools should refrain from emphasizing on profit making alone as it gives a sense of a one dimensional outlook to young students, that incurring a loss is a curse. In reality, in the corporate world, failure and loss making are inevitable.

The Capital Market without loss is like Christianity without hell. Instead they should teach students how to buy a business, how to value a business—not just on how to determine the price of a business.

Because price is what you pay, whereas value is what you get. Their perception should be positioned to accept losses in business as a part of the business itself and not be viewed as a point of failure.

Never be a prisoner of the past,
be an architect of future...
because then and only then
Will you have the ability to move
from one failure to another
With renewed enthusiasm

In Organizations, that I have had the pleasure of managing, we have always had one simple principle for everyone in the Company; *Compensation through Contribution,* irrespective of their position in the Company.

Habit # 4

Chasing the Business NOT Attracting it—Working IN or ON the Business

Are you working **IN** the business or **ON** the business? Are you chasing the business or learning to attract it? Most Entrepreneurs believe that no one can do it better than them. They think that substantial time is wasted explaining things to others. This leads them into attempting to doing everything themselves—all the time. These Entrepreneurs are working **IN** the business.

As General George S. Patton would say "Never tell people how to do things. Tell them what to do and they will surprise you with their ingenuity".

Entrepreneurs must learn the art of working **ON** the business, for then and only then will the business grow and even prosper.

When opportunity knocks you better be ready. Remember, when others see obstacles real Entrepreneurs see opportunity. And this can only happen when one is working **ON** the business.

A successful businessman's daughter married a good for nothing guy and the father had a meeting with his new son-in-law. "I love my daughter, and now I welcome you into the family," said the man. "To show how much we care for you, I've made you a 50-50 partner IN my business. All you have to do is go to the factory every day and learn the operations."

The son-in-law said, "I hate factories. I can't stand the noise." "I see," replied the father-in-law. "Well, then you can work in the office and take

Failure is the condiment
That gives success its flavor

charge of some of the operations." "I hate office work," said the son-in-law. "I can't stand being stuck behind a desk all day."

"Wait a minute," said the father-in-law. "I just gave you half interest IN a profitable business, but you don't like factories and won't work in an office. What am I going to do with you?"

"Easy," said the son-in-law..."Buy me out." (He was working ON the business)

Habit # 5

Doing the same thing over and over again, expecting a different result; be prepared to change course

If you really want to succeed, get creative and develop a sense of urgency in your life. Prepare to change course and re-evaluate.

We cannot solve problems using the same kind of thinking we used to create them in the first place. And most often it is very simple; get back to basics.

Continental airlines went from worst to first because the CEO convinced their employees that they could change course and be successful; and change course they did. They re-evaluated their strengths, re-positioned their weaknesses and decided to start right from the basics.

Xerox, on the other hand, almost had 100% market share of the copier market and decided that they could make more money by simply selling more copiers. They expected that just by doing what they were doing, but just more of it, they would be successful.

Toshiba and Cannon entered the market place and took away almost 150% of the market right from under Xerox. How? They changed the way the copier industry market was perceived.

Every challenge
You have been through
Every adversity
You faced
Your character
Has been developed
Your strength
Has been increased
Your vision
Has been enlarged

You cannot have control over how the wind blows, but surely you can adjust the sails.

If you focus on results, you will never change; if you focus on change you will get results.

You can be on the right track and still get run over if you only sit there; be prepared to change.

Habit # 6
Strategic thinking without the Operational knowhow

However good the strategy, you should occasionally look at the results. This will determine how successful you were when you strategized.

When turning strategies into action never confuse effort with results, as effort is synonymous with activity, results are supported by action. And any strategy without the operational component cannot be successful.

Those that believe they are the 'big shots' and the epitome of strategy; and therefore strategize by themselves, leaving the operational aspects to another; are actually most often the cause of the team being unsuccessful.

Experiences have taught me that 'big shots' are actually the 'little shots' that just keep shooting.

Strategy and operations always go hand-in-hand.

The Navy was preparing to sink a decommissioned ship off the coast of Florida so as to create an artificial reef and a tourist diving attraction. They had invited the best strategists to help successfully plan this due to a possible environmental impact this could have on the area.

Countless hours were spent on the strategy to sink the ship, with little to no time being devoted to the operations or the execution.

I am often asked...
Why do you always take
the difficult road?
And my answer
Why do you assume
That I see two roads

Finally the demolition experts went aboard the ship to evaluate the situation. Before they could even finish, the ship sank on its own. It seems that the bottom of the ship had rusted to the point that the ship could no longer remain afloat and sank in the worst possible place.

Fortune Magazine has estimated that 70% of all strategies fail.

Failure often occurs because ineffective planning methods are used to turn strategies into executable projects.

And this normally happens when they team that does the strategizing does not involve the team that will operate and execute the project.

Planning must clearly align projects with strategic and operational intent to boost the odds of success.

Habit # 7
Conservative Behavior; when you are in business stick your neck out and risk it

As James B. Conant once said, "Behold the turtle. He makes progress only when he sticks his neck out".

People have potential beyond their wildest imagination. Most people can do extraordinary things only if they learned to take risks. Yet most people don't. They just watch life go by as if it would last forever.

Don't be afraid to go out on a limb—that's where the fruit is. In a day, when you don't come across any problems, you can be sure you are travelling in a wrong path.

A classic example of risk taking is Wal-Mart. They stuck their neck out and competed with some of the best with only one huge risk taking strategy; affordable product at an affordable price. They kept their prices low and increased volume by getting people addicted to their strategy.

Take charge of your life
And be prepared
To change course

McDonalds was determined to take a risk and set the price of a burger such that they would make less money from one burger but sell millions in multiple countries. Their strategy also worked successfully.

In both cases they stuck their neck out and took risks.

Progress always involves risk. As Frederick B. Wilcox would say, "You can't steal second base and keep your foot on first". The more chance there is of stubbing your toe the more chance you have of stepping into success.

Erica Jong sums this up very well when she says "And the trouble is, if you don't risk anything, you risk even more".

Talking of taking risks reminds me of a shoe factory that sent two marketing scouts in a region in South Africa to study the prospects for expanding business.

The first scout sent back a message that read "situation hopeless; no one here wears shoes". The second one wrote with great enthusiasm, "glorious business opportunity; they have no shoes".

It all depends on your thinking and how much you are willing to risk.

If someone feels that they never made a mistake in their life, then it means they never tried a new thing in their life.

All of us are born geniuses but some of us are more brain damaged than others. We are always told more about our limitations than about our potential and that is why when most of us go to our graves, we take our music with us.

We need to look to the future with a larger vision, one that pushes us towards taking chances and risks. We need to push the envelope.

Our elders used to say; Old habits die hard. I say old habits never die; we just need to deal with them. In order to understand

Involve your people
In decision making
And the results
Will surprise you

where an Entrepreneur can go, it is important to understand where he has been.

Habits are like shadows; they will always follow you wherever you go.

So develop good habits, stay the course and remember dear Entrepreneur; we need to think before we act, plan before we execute, try before we give up and most importantly risk before we expect reward.

Remember... No Guts, No Glory!

CHAPTER 5

Should an Entrepreneur go Solo or Adopt a Partner

A Partnership
Is a Promise made
And a Promise kept

The Partnership Pledge

Confucius has said "Those whose ways are different do not make plans together". So very true indeed!

In reality, there are various attributes that need to be considered before one can decide on whether to operate one's own business, or partner with another. And experiences in the world of business have pros and cons to each side.

In my opinion and experience, the question to rather ask is "am I capable of running the business and that too on my own". And if the answer is yes, then solo is certainly the way to go.

Let me emphasize again, that there is no definitive answer to the direction in which an Entrepreneur should lean; it depends on loads of factors and conditions, and is unique to each individual and their situation.

But one thing is certain… a friendship founded on business is better and much stronger than a business founded on friendship.

Great partnerships can be exceedingly rewarding. Think of the Beatles— John Lennon and Paul McCartney, or for that matter the dancers— Fred Astaire and Ginger Rogers. Each brought complementary skills to the partnership that allowed them to achieve more than they could have ever achieved by themselves.

Because of the need for conciliation and the dynamics of collective influence that comes along with sharing a business, a partnership can be very difficult to maintain and run effectively.

As Lee Iacocca has so correctly said, "the first requisite in running a good business is the ability to collaborate with good people". Therefore the single most important decision an Entrepreneur has to make when forming a partnership is the choice of a partner.

Before you decide
To engage
A business partner
Learn to differentiate
Between
Essential and Priority

Worldly experiences dictate that you should only take on a partner if you 'absolutely' need that person's money or expertise. As an alternative, get the money as a loan or hire the person as a consultant to fill that need.

Our thinking gets swayed by people who are fine professionals and we automatically deduce that they will become good business partners. Wrong! Just because a person is good in the professional circuit, does not necessarily mean he is a good businessman. In fact, my experiences have proven otherwise.

My First Partnership Catastrophe

In my world of Entrepreneurship, I have had several personal experiences, some of them being horribly disastrous.

The mistake I made then was helping another person start a business, capitalizing the entire business (my partner had no money to invest… or at least that is what he told me), entrusting my partner with the reins of the business, and trusting his intentions before putting him through the test. I even gave him absolute authority to run the business (and for that matter to run it to the ground), with few to no controls in place.

I accepted the fact that he would take care of the business and expected him to be 'fair' to me as a partner. After all I had enabled him to establish his own business. I was so naïve and completely foolish. This was my first ever real business relationship and a very costly lesson was learned from this partnership.

The words of my friend, philosopher and guide, Noshir Dubash immediately haunted me, for he had said, "this world is very transactional, and extremely unforgiving. Trust no one in business for they will use you till they need you; after that you will be history".

And history I was; lost $75,000 in equity, had to pay unpaid suppliers and creditors from personal monies, and had to deal with the bank,

Choosing the right Partner
For your business
Is like choosing your Life Partner

as my partner abandoned the business, took all the money and fled the country.

This episode taught me that emotions and misplaced sympathies have no place in any partnership or commerce, and that as a businessman, I should think first from the head and then from the heart. I blame myself for this ordeal as my partner (I detest referring to him as such), had no 'skin in the game' and no controls to adhere to.

I allowed him to work off a platform that was destined to succeed only on personal integrity and moral values, which I quickly learned, were two of the least sought after ingredients in my partnership, at least from his side that is.

Choosing a Partner

Human relationships are extremely complex and grossly misunderstood. A wrong business partner can not only ruin you financially but can also quickly convert you into a complete emotional wreck. Get the point!

Partnerships are not successful on a *need based* basis. They require acts of courage; courage to take tough decisions together, courage to face challenges together and the courage to stand up against any attack on the business, the partnership and the partners.

To be in partnership is to blend in and become one. Remember the motto of the Musketeers; *One for all and all for one.*

The situation gets even more complex if there are multiple partners in the business; two egos are somewhat tolerable and workable—more than two are dangerous, can be very difficult to handle and may result in a 'you' versus 'them' syndrome.

If an Entrepreneur decides that forming a partnership is the best choice (I would urge you to think again, just one more time before you choose), then pay heed to some vital consideration before selecting a partner.

Never test the depth
Of a river
With both feet

Trust Honesty and Integrity

The nastiest part in a partnership is when one partner has to constantly look over his shoulder to reassure himself that he is not being compromised.

Trust, honesty and integrity are vital values in any business relationship and should be understood upfront by both sides.

Partnerships are based on trust, and trust is like oxygen for a business partnership. To gain experience and understand the relationship, we all go through toe-wetting experiences before we jump in, head first.

Promises kept, expectations met and confidence in the abilities of the other, all contribute towards allowing us to wade deeper into the relationship.

And talking of testing relationships, remember and follow that age old saying; ... go one step at a time.

If a partnership is to succeed, partners must check their egos at the door.

Power always poses a unique test in a partnership. The challenge is then to be honest about one's limitations, capabilities and skills.

Expectations

We all have expectations in our relationships—whether with parents, spouses, children, siblings, friends or business partners. Expectations are those tools that avoid all the 'you should have known it' in our lives.

Sharing and shouldering responsibilities, and 'filling in' for your partner, are vital considerations and tacit expectations for a successful partnership.

I have been involved with theatre since I was 6 years old and have written, directed, produced and acted in several plays.

A clearly communicated expectation
Will surely be met

While performing one of my plays, the 'set' of our scene was about to collapse, while the play was in progress. One of the ropes that held up the 'walls' of our stage set got loose and the set was about to crumble in.

That would have been quite a disaster and extremely embarrassing. Everyone panicked, except those two people backstage that had designed and constructed the entire set.

Before the play began they knew their role and my expectations; the set had to be 'up' throughout the play and would be brought 'down' only after the performance.

Both of them ran up to the wall of our 'set' that was about to collapse, and with the use of a few chairs on which they stood, held the entire set 'up' for a whole hour till the play finally concluded. And they did it so well that no one even knew what was going on behind the scenes.

Our expectations were very clear and were adhered to, though I cannot show enough appreciation for what they both accomplished. They had expectations set in advance, and all they did was following them as diligently as they possibly could.

There are three distinct parts to successful partnership expectations.

- First, expectations need to be clear and need to be documented and understood by each partner; the more vagueness and ambiguity the more chance for later anguish
- Second, is doing what you say you are going to do; adherence to the expectation
- Third, measurement of the expectation; this is where the rubber meets the road.

Vision for the Enterprise & Goals for the Business

A very important point to ascertain is whether your partner shares the same vision as you, or do they hope only to be able to make a decent

If you are ready
And can do it
Then go ahead
And do it...
Alone

living out of one business with fewer responsibilities than would be actually required.

The biggest drawback in having a partner is the vision that is being set for the enterprise, and the execution of that vision with the pace that is envisioned.

An Entrepreneur that goes solo can start today, but if he partners with another, has to wait till the other is ready.

First of all, you have to give up absolute control of the business and learn to compromise.

And when major decisions have to be made, such as whether or how to expand the business, partners often disagree on the best course and are left with a potentially explosive situation.

Such predicaments are not predictable and therefore cannot be anticipated; they just have to be dealt with as they occur.

Roles

Sometimes the biggest challenge for a partner is to come to grips with his role in the partnership.

Whenever I'm disappointed with my spot in life, I stop and think about our son Kyrus, when, for the very first time, he was trying out for a part in the school play in Kindergarten. My wife, Persis, told me that he'd set his heart on being in it, though she feared because he was shy, then, he would not be chosen.

On the day the parts were awarded, I went with her to collect him after school. Kyrus rushed up to us, eyes shining with pride and excitement. "Guess what, Mom, Dad," he shouted, and then said those words that will remain a lesson to me all my life......"I got a part in the play; I've been chosen to clap and cheer."

*A Partnership is only as Strong as the
Weakest Partner*

Talk about role acceptance and a positive attitude!

Personalities of partners can do substantial incremental damage if partners and their roles are not compatible. If a partner panics at every hurdle encountered, then more time is spent in convincing than in solving the issue.

If a partner cannot cope with stress then his role cannot be one of decision making as it will only tend to result in impulsive action.

It is very sensible and extremely critical to conclude what role each partner intends to play in the business. And this is generally determined by the skill level of each partner.

For a partnership to be successful, roles must not only be compatible but also complementary.

Leadership Styles

From time in memoriam the age old question still continues, are Leaders born, or are they made. I believe that with inherent qualities, they are born, but also made. Leadership does not suddenly dawn on a person. It is the situation that they fall in that releases the true potential of the person and helps him soar like an eagle.

The world has shown us time and again that some are born great, some achieve greatness and some have greatness thrust upon them.

As Joseph E. Brooks has said, "Show me a country, a Company or an organization that is doing well and I'll show you a good Leader".

- Leadership is not so much about technique and methods as it is about opening the heart
- Leadership is about inspiration; of oneself and of others
- Great Leadership is about human experiences, not processes

A Leader is a Dealer in Hope...
Everybody cannot be a Leader

- Leadership is not a formula or program; it is a human activity that comes from the heart and considers the hearts of others
- Great Leadership is an attitude, not a routine
- Leaders are givers, not takers of positive energy
- Leaders are in total charge of their destiny. No excuses given and none tolerated

For a partnership to function effectively and continue on successfully there can be only one Leader. If not, then conflict will overtake cooperation and the partnership cannot progress successfully. The dominant partner must have the ability and the finesse to involve the other partner in the operations of the corporation in a less threatening way.

He must also be able to take on more responsibility. After all responsibilities always gravitate to the person that can shoulder them. The other partner must be able to feel adequate enough to want to be a part of the enterprise.

This type of Leadership style also helps to establish a very clear understanding of roles and responsibilities in a partnership. It also establishes the fact that management is different from Leadership.

Communication

My nephew Naushad Buchia asked me a question during one of my trips to Mumbai, India, where my wife Persis and I went to attend the wedding ceremony of our niece and his sister Feroza.

"What is the one ingredient", he asked, "that you would rate above all else that would enable an Entrepreneur to be successful?"

And I answered without hesitation; 'Communication'.

One of the key factors to mastering your life is to master your communication.

"Management
Is doing things right,
Leadership
Is doing the right things"

Peter Drucker

The reason why most people have unsatisfactory results in their life is because they have poor communication skills. People get frustrated when they don't get what they want and often times don't realize it is because they did not communicate clearly, what it is they wanted. Poor results come from poor communication.

If you can get your point of view across in a language that can be understood and accepted by another, then more than half your job is done.

Effective communication is a two way street. It involves articulating your message so that it can be well understood, and active listening so that you may accept constructive feedback. It is all about conveying your message to other people clearly and unambiguously.

There are many elements that go into positive effective communication. They are verbal and non-verbal.

In my opinion, communication involves four key ingredients. And if any one of these is out of whack, the message can be completely misconstrued.

a) The words we choose

The words that we choose to use when we communicate have tremendous power. It can normalize and improve situations (if the right words are used) or it can be indeed very damaging (if incorrect words are selected and uttered). Choose your words with the intent of making your message clear and precise.

Lengthy dissertations and circuitous explanations are confusing to the listener and the message loses its concreteness, relevance, and impact.

b) How we say those words

The words that we use only make up 7 percent of our communication. The other 93 percent is voice tone and body language. What that means is, before you have even said a word, you have already said a lot. It is very important to practice paying attention to your voice tone.

*You will always deliver Superior
performance
If you learn do develop
Excellent communication*

It is important to be aware of your voice tone, when you speak. Have you ever had someone ask you for something in a whiny sounding voice; or how about in a very demanding tone of voice?

Think back to when someone has approached you with either of these voice tones. Did you really want to give them what they were asking for? Probably not, as you were turned off by their approach. Having a friendly confident tone can be very effective.

c) Our body language

Body language is huge! So many people are giving the wrong signals and they don't even realize it. Your words and voice tone may be saying one thing, but your body is saying something very different.

The non verbal speaks louder than the verbal, always. The person that you are communicating with will most often not even realize that they are being affected by your body language, however they are, it happens on a subconscious level.

d) The art of listening

How many of us actually hear what people are really saying. Listening is one of the most important skills you can posses. How well you choose to listen, will determine and strengthen your relationship with a person. By becoming a better listener, you will improve your ability to influence, persuade and negotiate.

Be deliberate with your listening and remind yourself constantly that your goal is to truly hear what the other person is saying. God has given us two ears and one mouth, so listen more than you speak!

Lack of communication is like whispering to the deaf or winking at the blind, and can put a serious strain on any relationship.

Most of a partnership's problems are matters of communication.

The greatest area for immense potential and also for a severe collapse is communication.

How you say
What you say
Really matters

Partners do not have to necessarily agree on every decision. They should communicate their differences in a constructive way that enables the business to move forward and improve upon what any of the owners could have done independently.

Talking of misconstrued communication—a little boy was attending his first wedding ceremony. After the service, his mother asked him, "So now that you have witnessed your first wedding, tell me son, how many women can a man marry?" "Sixteen," the boy responded.

His mother was amazed that he had an answer so quickly. "Well and how do you know that young man?" "Easy," the little boy said. "I was paying attention Mom. All you have to do is add it up, like the pastor communicated to us right now; 4 better, 4 worse, 4 richer, 4 poorer".

Most serious controversies that arise in a partnership are the direct result of misunderstanding. And inadequate or lack of communication is the catalyst that gives rise to misunderstanding.

Communication is that immutable barrier in a partnership between the thoughts of one partner verses another.

Put that handshake in writing

Remember that old saying, "I see... I understand, I do... I remember, I write... I accept". Oral agreements are the cause of most partnership issues, especially when the going gets tough.

Put all your agreements in writing.

Read them well, understand them, put pen to paper, agree on the final print, and then start working on the business with the expectation that you will never again need to look at those agreements.

In my final analysis, selecting a partner is most often a matter of intuition, you either feel good about the person or you simply don't. And if you don't, do not sign up under any circumstances.

More than 70% of Leadership
depends on communication

Remember, in life as in business, you can never change a person. You will ultimately land up changing yourself, trying to adapt to your partner and his ways of working.

And that is not good for the business or for your personal peace of mind. Whether to select a partner or not is simply a matter of skills and need.

In my opinion if you do not need to have a partner, you should most certainly not!

CHAPTER 6

The Silent Partner... the Entrepreneur's Spouse

We make them cry
Who care for us,

We cry for those
Who never care for us,

And...

care for those
will never cry for us

How silent is your Silent Partner

In this ever-evolving world of uncertainty and constant change, never ever doubt the influence of the Entrepreneur's Spouse, as most successful Entrepreneurs consider unconditional support from their spouses the single most important factor for their continued success.

Substantial research, extensive analysis and several personal interviews with successful Entrepreneurs and their spouses, has lead me to conclude that Entrepreneurs that come home to criticism and unpleasantness abandon their venture altogether.

It has also led me to the fact that Entrepreneurs easily change strategies if it is causing a problem at home.

If you glance through history books, you will notice that from time-in-memorial, behind every successful individual, there almost always has been a very dynamic spouse, standing side by side, ready to support, ready to give and most importantly, ready to act.

I have realized through personal experiences and also in the course of interaction with several Entrepreneurs, that a spouse can either make a person or break a person.

They have that power.

Let us attempt to understand the role of this very powerful individual that is probably the closest person in the life of an Entrepreneur, because a spouse is directly affected by the success or failure of the enterprise.

In the case of a business partner, their role in the business is most often direct and contractual, and, in most cases, is seen and acknowledged. On the other hand, a spouse frequently remains in the background, unstudied and generally unacknowledged.

Involve your
Significant other
In your
Decision making process

Is an Entrepreneurs Spouse really valued?

Entrepreneurs' spouses live with uncertainty. Most folks married to Entrepreneurs, value the role they play in supporting their partners' passion, and would want their spouse to embrace a less mercenary view of their relationship.

A necklace for a missed holiday dinner or a week away from home on business, when there happens to be a very sick child at home does not always go down very well with a spouse. Be optimistic, positive and generally not prone to worry and BINGO you're the Entrepreneurs version of a rock star.

As Peter F. Drucker has so pertinently said, and I quote, "Wherever you see a successful businessman, someone once made a courageous decision". And in most cases that courageous decision was either made or strongly influenced by the spouse. If they are your significant other, won't their opinion be significant as well?

There is often a disagreement about the answer to this question though my personal feeling and experience is YES INDEED... as their wisdom will sharpen your business skills at seeing things you would otherwise miss out on.

It is just like Wall Street, where people alight from a Rolls Royce to get advice from people who use the public transport system. A spouse can most often become the motivating and balancing factor in the life of an Entrepreneur.

According to Bibby Financial Services, spouses of business owners in the UK spend 230 million unpaid hours each month to help their partners' businesses. The report also shows that the hours worked by Entrepreneurs' partners are worth £72 billion every year to the UK economy. Something to think about!

Never Question your Spouse's Judgment...
Look who she Married

The Entrepreneurs PRENUP

Entrepreneurs remain positive about investing in people as most of them are of the belief that people are their greatest investors (remember, we discussed this earlier).

Does that include the spouse? And the flip side of this is a question that is not very often asked (as it interferes with the family life and ego of a spouse)—would you ever hire your spouse either as an independent consultant or an employee in your business?

Life as an Entrepreneur is complicated enough to start with, and the added burden of balancing business and family is not something an Entrepreneur ever looks forward to… not even when things are going good.

To create the business of your dreams, an Entrepreneur must learn the ins and outs of an Entrepreneurial partnership; survival with the spouse, while focusing on growing and managing a business.

Opening a business is one thing, growing it is another.

When we put two people together, life becomes intricate, problems get knotty and the solution gets even more challenging. As has been rightly said, "True partnership means becoming comfortable with compromise, but not becoming compromising".

Your partnership should be committed towards harmonizing the freedom and vision of your Entrepreneurial dreams with the grounded practicality of making a business work together.

And talking about commitment, there was a striking difference however that I instantly observed when interviewing women Entrepreneurs. It also resonated with the fact that the instinctive nurturing feeling in a woman usually dominates her personality.

Believe in your spouse...
They will help you achieve
The impossible

I observed that in order of priority, women Entrepreneurs usually list their spouse first, their close friends second and their business associates third. INTERESTING! (Men … are we listening).

Spouses of Entrepreneurs feel like second class citizens when compared to the business venture. They are asked to 'balance' the home and the Entrepreneurial venture to such an extent, they feel that they are always asked to 'accommodate' with the assurance that things will only get better—the question being WHEN!

They believe in their Entrepreneur and the business, and are willing to 'please' to such a degree, that sometimes they just wait for a miracle to happen.

But do they really understand the business and what it takes to be successful? Can they represent their Entrepreneur and the business at a social gathering, or are they at times a source of embarrassment.

Prerequisites to Being a Silent partner

Let us address and understand my five non-compromise-able prerequisites to being a 'silent partner'.

The Balancing Act—Bad feedback and white lies

People like to be nice to people. But unfortunately, when it comes to business, spouses don't always give the best advice.

This is especially true at the birth of a business. Nobody wants to be a buzz-kill. The spouse hesitates to tell the Entrepreneur their idea is bad, or their planning is not adequate, or anything else negative. Most spouses get conditioned to be supportive regardless of the situation.

They also do not want to be wrong. Imagine your Entrepreneur has an idea that you think is terrible. You share your objections, but he goes ahead with the idea anyways, and it succeeds. Now you'll always be the naysayer that never believed in them. Nobody wants to be that person.

A supportive spouse
Is like a rock...
Immovable

And that is exactly why most often you rarely get honest, objective business advice from spouses. And yet, spouses are the first people Entrepreneurs turn to for advice.

Confidence v/s Acceptance—Is knowledge and confidence, confused with emotion and acceptance

Emotional support is really necessary but logical balance is very fundamental. And emotions normally lead to acceptance. It is important that a spouse understand the Entrepreneur and the business well enough to be supportive in the right way.

A hypothetical situation was created where 10 aviation Entrepreneurs and their respective spouses were asked to board an airplane and were told that the flight that they were about to take was the first-ever to feature pilotless technology.

Each one of the couples was then told, privately, that their Company's software was running the aircraft's automatic pilot system.

Nine of the Entrepreneurs and their respective spouses promptly left the aircraft, each offering a different type of excuse.

One Entrepreneur and his spouse alone remained on board the jet, seeming very calm indeed.

Asked why they were so confident in this first pilotless flight, the spouse of the Entrepreneur replied: "If it is the same software that is developed by our Company's IT systems department, this plane won't even take off"!

Pushing or Nagging... which one is it

There is a very fine difference between being *pushed* and being *nagged*. In such a case only the receiver knows the actual difference. It also depends on the receiver's level of tolerance.

This Life is not a
Dress rehearsal Dear Husband
It is the real thing...
Better get used to it

Persis Buchia

Some Entrepreneurs that I have had the pleasure of speaking with have told me in no uncertain language, that ego has a big role to play when an Entrepreneur interacts with the spouse. Entrepreneurs believe that they know more than their spouse and therefore cannot stomach direct criticism or *nagging* as they prefer to call it.

For the spouse on the other hand it is simply a very normal interaction between two spouses. They forget, at times, that *pushing* can be construed as *nagging* especially when the Entrepreneur suddenly decides to wear the *Entrepreneur's hat* just during that very conversation.

It is the finesse and nurturing possessed by the spouse that is essential in such a situation. Sometimes spouses push harder than they should because of social reasons. A friend's partner is doing so well in business that it compels the spouse to push her Entrepreneur to achieve just that little bit more. These situations can cause nothing but conflict and can lead the Entrepreneur to be miserable and insecure.

Determination and Persistence—How much is too much

Everybody has a dream and the hope that they will certainly succeed. But is that all that is required for success? A vision for the future is the first step in the right direction, but is certainly not the only step.

The will to succeed is a direct result of *focus on action*. But the will to be able to succeed is born from determination and persistence.

We are all unique—that is our strength. And with our minds and the right use of our inner strength, we can almost make anything happen. But we all need the comfort that we have support from people that really care.

I asked a 'silent partner' once—"Your Entrepreneur has failed twice already—why are you still supporting his business venture—do you really believe this time he will succeed—haven't you had enough already"?

If your Silent Partner
Is too silent
There may be
A really good reason for it

And she replied with conviction in her voice, "Swimming along the flow is effortless but swimming against it needs effort. You should not go the way life takes you, but take life the way you want to go…. dare to be determined and persistent. This time I will be helping him succeed"!

Are you IN or OUT of the Business—What is your Commitment

In my opinion and experience, the biggest question of all that an Entrepreneurs spouse needs to answer is—are you in or out of the business. And this by no means is an easy question to answer.

But once you have decided that you are IN the business, it becomes a ball-and-chain that you carry with you for a long time, whether you like it or not. You are then married not only to the Entrepreneur but also to the business.

In my world of Entrepreneurship, my spouse, Persis, is certainly IN the business. Though her frustrations are very real and sometimes visible; the unconditional support and caring, the constant concern for my accomplishments and my success, and the worry regarding an adverse effect on my ego, far make up for her dissatisfaction and irritation of the Entrepreneurial situation.

Having said this, she is also my best and worst critic; a role that I encourage her to play for continued success of the business.

In the words of Eleanor Roosevelt, "I think I've been asked to do something about everything in the world except change the weather". These words so aptly describe the feelings of an Entrepreneur's spouse.

There are always competing needs, and constant juggling is required so as to prioritize and focus to find a fine balance.

Business ownership can cause strain and resentment, spouses say. It's almost like there's a third-party in your marriage.

Social acceptance of a spouse
Is the biggest support
For an Entrepreneur

Work-life balance is one of the biggest concerns for Entrepreneurs, and often it's up to the spouse to keep that harmony.

The Entrepreneurial Dilemma

Conflict causes unreasonable actions that could derail the Entrepreneurial path for an Entrepreneur. It is not easy to balance work and home life, and the added pressure from the spouse forces one to take a decision as to the way forward.

During one of my recent motivational speaking trips to Dubai and India, I had the pleasure of interacting with a budding Entrepreneur that is faced with the dilemma of continuing his business or going back to a regular job.

He has quite the passion and the commitment and also has enough steady business coming his way. He does not have the time to grow his business as he is holding on to his day job for security reasons, and is working on his business part time, thereby leaving no time for the family.

His spouse wants him to spend more time with her and their daughter and is not very eager with the fact that he is building a business that gets them financial stability because they are at present financial very stable. His spouse does not want him to give up his day job either.

So what should he do? Due to home pressures and the added guilt of not spending enough time with the family, he is struggling with the decision of whether to grow and give up his steady job, or to give up his dream and go back to his job.

The struggle is one between family pressures, personal guilt and the pursuing of a dream as an Entrepreneur.

This is how they feel.... Our Silent Partners

I consider myself privileged to have been invited into the minds and hearts of our 'silent partners'. What I learned has certainly made

Avoid Conflict at all Costs
It will be to the
Ultimate benefit
Of your Dreams

me think about my own situation much more than I would ever care to admit.

One final question that I asked them all—"having gone through the pleasure of being called 'the silent partner', and having unconditionally supported your significant other's Entrepreneurship dreams and ventures, if there was just one thing you wanted to tell 'your Entrepreneur' what would it be"?

Their feelings, experiences and choice of words may have been quite different based on their circumstances, but one common message was echoed loud and clear, and I paraphrase this for your reading.

"It is a very difficult and challenging path but indeed a satisfying one. It is also a lonely experience which many will never be able to relate to—however, it is a journey worth pursuing. My Dear Entrepreneur, It is important to remember that life goes on. While building a business please don't put your spouse on hold".

CHAPTER 7

Is Entrepreneurship Hereditary

Remember...

The Rung of the Ladder
Was never meant to rest upon...

But to hold one's Foot
Long enough

To enable him to put the other
Foot a little bit higher

Genetic behavior... does it really exist

According to a Ewing Marion Kauffman Foundation report released in the summer of 2009, "Nearly half of new business founders had a parent who started a small business first. Slightly more than 15% had siblings who launched a business before they did."

In other words, Entrepreneurism may run in families.

Also in the article: "'If you had a family member who started a business, you are more likely to become an Entrepreneur than someone who didn't," says Vivek Wadhwa, founder of two technology companies, as well as a senior research associate at the Labor & Worklife Program at Harvard Law School and a co-author of the Kauffman study. "They provide inspiration, financing and teach you the ropes".

But I still do believe that you have to do your own growing, no matter how tall your father was.

And remember, our kids are watching us.

I have recently become aware of the influence I was having on our son Kyrus when, after a business call, he turned to me and said, "Dad, I like hearing how you talk on the phone. Will I be able to do that some day?" It was a simple, but powerful, statement.

Children learn what they see and hear. And our boy is learning to run a business just by watching me. I'm glad that he is being exposed to business ownership as an option for himself in the future.

I've told him that I learned much of what I needed to know to run a business by working for someone else first. And I've also told him that I started to plan to work for myself while I was still working for someone else. Both things made my transition to Entrepreneur easier.

As you embrace the possibilities of being an Entrepreneur, consider using your time to show your kids about the benefits of being self-

When you live
For a strong purpose
Hard work is not an option
It is a necessity

employed. They can learn a lot just by watching and listening to you. Invite them into your work space.

Let them help when they can. Show them that though the buck stops with you, you also have a lot of freedom and flexibility. And, if you're lucky enough to love what you do, let them see the value of passion and enthusiasm in work.

Entrepreneurship—The Indian way

The Indian society has historically evolved on the principle of hereditary occupations, where the choice of occupation was absent for most people. Occupations were just not inherited in the family; rather a caste was identified with the hereditary occupation.

Sometimes even the name of the caste corresponded with the occupation. The son was inducted into the father's occupation at a very early age. He had very little choice but to take over the reins of the family business. The son of a blacksmith would become nothing but a blacksmith.

Though the British colonial intervention was a major factor that transformed the Indian society in a definite way, it was only after India gained independence that the pace of industrialization really picked up. Transformation of artisan production into modern enterprise led to empowerment thus breaking the barrier of restriction on the choice of occupation.

Globalization has given a big boost to traditional occupations and businesses. I believe that today there are more Entrepreneurs in India than anywhere in the world. Indian Entrepreneurs are making waves all across the world and spreading their tentacles in various corners of the globe.

Jamsetji Tata (founder of India's biggest business house), G. D. Birla (a visionary with a rebellious attitude for success), Dhirubhai Ambani (the most enterprising Indian Entrepreneur), are classic examples of Entrepreneurs that started small but with a big vision. These individuals

There are two ways
Of facing diffi culties...
You alter the difficulties
Or you alter yourself
To meet them

have spurred the growth of Indian businesses and the economic agenda of the country.

And over time their sons and daughters, through modern technology and extensive education, have taken these Organizations to new and even greater heights. But they could do this solely because of the foundations developed by their fathers.

The Indian Dabawallas (Tiffin Carriers)

For those of you that do not know of their existence, the 'Dabawallas' (Tiffin Carriers) of Mumbai (formerly Bombay), are the most studied Entrepreneurs in Management Schools across the Globe. And YES their business has been very proudly passed down from father to son.

Wherever you may be staying or working in Mumbai, in this largest Indian metropolis of over 20 million people, you never ever fail to receive home food in time for lunch. Thanks to the network of Dabawallas, that has been functioning in an amazing way for more than 100 years and recognized by management gurus as the best case of Entrepreneurship and network management in the world.

This is the saga of the Nutan Tiffin Box Suppliers Charity Trust better known as 'Dabawallas'—the carrier guy who picks up the lunch-box in the morning and unfailingly delivers it on time to your place of work, anywhere in Mumbai, at a highly economic price.

Daily about 300,000 meals are delivered by this system at an average cost of about Rs. 450 (US $ 10) per month.

Some may find his task trivial in the overall scheme of things but his clients will willingly testify on the importance of daily receiving home-cooked food, so lovingly cooked by the mother, wife or sister at their place of work.

You can't fail to marvel at their system, with an annual turnover of Rs. 50,000,000 (US $ 10 million) and 4,500 carriers who meet

Do not ask
To lower your targets
Ask to more get Ammunition
To meet them

and exchange Tiffin-boxes at public places like railway stations, etc. without ever causing a jam or any confusion—just like a well-oiled Olympic relay team.

Lunch-boxes are sorted and exchanged in a jiffy, with zero documentation involved. Yet, rarely has it happened that a lunch has missed its destined belly.

Though most of the Tiffin-carriers are illiterate, they are the ultimate practitioners of logistics management like the apostles of the hub-and-spoke game plan, Just-in-Time tactics and Supply Chain Management principles. They seem to be following these strategies long before these terms were even coined.

And all this information and expertise has been passed down the family, very proudly. While in Mumbai during our last visit, I had the privilege of speaking to a Dabawalla whilst travelling in a local train—"How do you guys do it", I asked. "Very simple", was his answer. "We follow what we have been taught, believe in the indigenous operating system as it has been designed by our Seniors, and most importantly never try and fix that which has been working so fine".

And then he told me something that I believe we have forgotten in our quest for Entrepreneurship and business success—"Our success is measured by only one thing", he said, "getting hot food in time to the designated cold stomach". WOW—what a mission statement; so simple yet so powerful.

The history of Tiffin box carriers run parallel to the history of Mumbai's development. Saddled with growing population in the late19th century, new settlements further from the old Fort complex started cropping up in Mumbai.

As residential colonies kept moving further from the Fort, a lot of office goers started finding it difficult to go home for their lunch in the afternoons. Carrying lunch boxes while leaving home in the morning was not exactly fashionable.

Your mind is like a Parachute
It Functions only when Open

In 1890 a wealthy businessman working in downtown Mumbai employed a young man to fetch his lunch every afternoon. As time went by, business picked up through referrals and soon the pioneer Tiffin-carrying Entrepreneur had to call for more helping hands from his family.

Though there were no umbrella Organizations for the carriers then, the first informal attempt to unionize was made by Mahadev Havji Bacche in 1930.

A charitable trust was registered n 1956 under the name of "Nutan Mumbai Tiffin Box Suppliers Trust". Even today every carrier is expected to contribute Rs 45 (US $ 1) per month towards the trust. The commercial arm was registered quite later in 1968 as "Mumbai Tiffin Box Carriers Association".

And YES, even today these Entrepreneurs pass on from father to son, their business expertise and human behavioral wisdom and interaction.

Classifying Hereditary Entrepreneurship

In my opinion, hereditary Entrepreneurship can be divided into three categories:

Business Families

The first category is that of well established *'Business Families'*. They have a strong base, with most individuals following the family business tradition passed on from generation to generation. Most of these Organizations have a strong management team, and are now going global.

A classic example is that of the Ambani brothers; Mukesh Ambani (5th richest man in the world) and Anil Ambani (6th richest man in the world). The brothers inherited their fortune from renowned industrialist Dhirubhai Ambani, a rags-to-riches business tycoon.

Nobody said Life would be Easy
They just promised
It would be Worth it

Young Graduates

The second category is dominated by *'Young Graduates'* that are an integral part of the Entrepreneurial business growth. With information technology and multinational corporations on the rise, these young Entrepreneurs serve as a backbone of many flourishing enterprises.

Their fathers before them were also once young Entrepreneurs; but progress has favored the newer generation thanks to the willingness to invest capital and fund start-ups.

Global education has given rise to this category of individuals.

Maverick Entrepreneurs

The third category of society is what I refer to as *'Maverick Entrepreneurs'*.

Entrepreneurship is in their blood. Educational qualifications do not mean much to them; rather they rely on sheer Entrepreneurship abilities that include training, customer service skills, networking, hard work and Innovation.

Most of the third world countries have this category of Entrepreneurs.

They pool their resources together and operate in what we refer to today as joint venturing. They are the 'unreasonable community', and I believe, that a lot of the world's progress depends on their kind.

Ethics v/s Survival

Hereditary Entrepreneurship, and especially the first category—*Business Families,* carry with it a huge load; that of continuation of the family tradition and business, and sustained expansion to maintain and nurture the family name.

The pressure here is to Preserve the Past, Protect the Present and Perfect the Future. And this strain can cause a severe challenge to the age old question in business—Ethics v/s Survival.

Always Seek to Achieve
Maximum Results
With Minimum Time

Most often it is the generation gap that poses a challenge. New ideas may seem impetuous and idealistic to the older generation. The younger generation may feel a sense of dinosaur-ism with the way business is handled and will want to revamp in a hurry.

That is where experience and maturity play a lead role in bridging the space.

And when it is a question of Survival, do Ethics really matter?

An older gentleman was on the operating table awaiting surgery. He insisted that his son, a renowned surgeon, perform the operation. The son was absolutely against performing the surgery as he felt that he may not be able to take critical decisions if the need arose during that time.

As the older gentleman was about to get the anesthesia, he asked to speak to his son. 'Yes Dad, what is it' asked the son. The father replied, 'Don't be nervous son. Do your best. And just remember, if it doesn't go well, if something happens to me, your mother is going to come and live with you and your wife....for the rest of your life!'

Talk about Maturity and Experience!

Generation gap is a major cause for business separation between the younger generation and the wiser generation. And by separation, I mean disjointed in the way we think—distinct thought processes.

Yes, I term us the wiser generation because experience teaches you what university degrees will simply not. This statement may not always be true, but to a large extent it has a proven track record of being precise.

Our fore-fathers started businesses with the idea of making money by promoting ethical business practices, moral behavior and responsible management in corporations and institutions. Technology has taken over the world and along with it also our thinking.

*Decisive People do not have
Pending Decisions*

Today we have far more analyzed data and available information at our disposal that gives us the flexibility to take quicker decisions and in the process allows us to short-circuit ethics and go straight for the money.

A program called 'Emerging issues and ethics' by the Markkula Center for Applied Ethics at the Santa Clara University, is an effort by students at 50 universities to have graduates sign a voluntary pledge to create value, responsibly and ethically.

The project has been termed 'The MBA Oath', and was picked up and promoted by a group of students at the Harvard Business School class of 2009. Only 40% of the class of 2009 at the Harvard Business School took the oath. The project was:

- To determine and recognize the role of a Business Leader in society
- Pioneer the idea of creating a corporate pledge and an organizational culture, regarding ethics and responsibility when governing Organizations

The pledge would establish that as a Business Leader, the person taking the oath would recognize their role in society; their purpose is to lead people, manage the resources and create value that no single individual can create alone.

There has been plenty of criticism on this MBA oath with management scholars emphasizing that the function of a Business Leader is much broader than simple serving the shareholders. The question that was also raised is what is the real effectiveness of such an oath?

The Other Side

Many Entrepreneurs would rather convince their offspring not to follow in their footsteps, but instead venture out and either find a job or get involved in another business undertaking other than the hereditary one.

Determine the critical aspects
Of your business
And stay focused on them

There can be multiple reasons for this maneuvering.

Entrepreneurs that are not successful in-spite of trying multiple times will always believe that grass has to be greener on the other side. Insecurity forces them to think differently, and a job, where money flows in every month in the form of a fixed salary amount, sounds very appealing and extremely safe.

Another reason for the advice to deviate from a hereditary business could simply be that the family business may have outlived its existence, and starting from scratch again may bring back memories of pain and suffering to the Entrepreneur.

Whatever the circumstances may be, I have come to believe and accept that Fear, Insecurity and Lack of proper guidance, are the cause of it all.

They are the main reasons that may entice a person to move away from embracing and continuing on the Entrepreneurial path to success, be it hereditary or otherwise.

CHAPTER 8

Is there really a Difference

Innovator

Leader

Businessman

Entrepreneur

Difference or Distinction

People generally use the words Innovator, Leader, Businessman and Entrepreneur interchangeably. Actually there is a distinction between these categories of people that needs to be acknowledged before one can really understand the differences. A common question that arises is can one person be recognized as fitting in a multiple of these categories.

Innovator

To me, an innovator is a pace setter, a trend setter; someone that modernizes the way it has always been done.

A great example would be Bill Gates of Microsoft. He revolutionized the world of information technology and set a new bar for the world to follow. His famous quote 'Your most unhappy customers are your greatest source of learning', should be a foundation of inspiration to Entrepreneurs for generations to come.

Another good example is that of Sergey Brin and Larry Page of Google. They not only converted the way the world searches for stuff on the internet, but did it in such a way that it is now called *googling* no matter which search engine one uses.

To me, these are people that have had the vision and the guts to change history by creating it themselves.

Leader

A Leader on the other hand, is a dealer in hope. He is a person that can inspire, motivate and get the best out of people no matter what language they speak or what culture they belong to. People willingly follow them and believe that they will handhold them throughout their journey and guide them to a successful end.

The great Indian Leader Mahatma Gandhi is one of the best examples of what a Leader can be; quietly stubborn yet richly effective. Single

Not-working is only
One letter away from
Net-working...
It's your choice

handedly and through his mantra of non-violence, he unified the people of India and compelled the British to leave and grant India her much deserved independence.

Colin Powell's admirable Leadership as Chairman of the Joint Chiefs of Staff, especially under such dire circumstances, and later United States Secretary of State, puts him in that category. His Leadership qualities inspired the US Army to march together as one.

Jack Welch of General Electric is another striking example of a great Leader. He took GE from where it was, to being recognized as the number one Company in the world during his tenure as Chief of the organization. What a journey for a man who joined the Company as a junior engineer and retired from the organization as the Chairman and CEO.

Businessman

The easiest way to describe a businessman is to mention the names JRD Tata of the TATA Group or Sam Walton of Wal-Mart or Warren Buffet of Berkshire Hathaway or Dhirubhai Ambani of Reliance Industries.

Each one of these businessmen has showed the world that nothing is beyond imagination. If you can dream of it you can achieve it for sure. If you really want it that bad you will surely get it. All you need is sheer Persistence, Perseverance and the Courage never to give up, no matter what the odds.

In my opinion, these are people that have developed the sense to make money by running businesses that are profitable and respected throughout the world.

Entrepreneur

When referring to Entrepreneurs, certain names immediately come to mind—Ray Kroc of McDonalds, Richard Branson of Virgin Airlines, Steve Jobs of Apple Computers and Thomas Watson of IBM.

Learn from the mistakes
Of others
Because you will not live
Long enough
To make all those mistakes yourself

These are individuals that have changed the industries that they worked in and have defined achievement by simply 'wanting so desperately to succeed'. They developed an unapologetic drive for profit which is the one essential factor in their success.

They have demonstrated to the world that failure is only temporary and one must learn to get up and move on.

These are risk taking visionaries that all have one thing in common; the burning desire to be successful. To them failure was never an option.

Entrepreneur, Innovator, Leader, Businessman

So the question is can an Entrepreneur be a Leader, an innovator, a businessman, or do these categories of people all possess different qualities that make them special in their own class.

For an Entrepreneur to be a Leader, he needs to have the energy of an Entrepreneur and the diplomacy of a Leader.

An Entrepreneur is Enthusiastic; a Leader is a Motivator. An Entrepreneur is a Visionary; a Leader is Tenacious. An Entrepreneur is a Risk-taker; a Leader is Inspiring. An Entrepreneur Organizes, Operates and assumes Risks; a Leader Rules, Guides and Inspires.

The DNA of these two types of people is very different. But what a dynamic person it would be if both these qualities of Entrepreneurship and Leadership were combined into one single person. If one could just think like an Entrepreneur and perform like a Leader, he could rule the world of business.

In my opinion, all Leaders are not Entrepreneurs. In fact in my experience, most are not. On the other hand most successful Entrepreneurs that I have had the privilege of interacting with are also gifted Leaders.

On the other hand, an innovator can also be an Entrepreneur. Innovation to me is not all about change. It is a process of creating, diffusing and

You have been bestowed with
Two Ears and One Mouth...
Use them in that proportion...

Listen More than you Speak

applying knowledge. To me, the Innovator stands between the Scientist and the Entrepreneur.

Invention, Innovation and Entrepreneurs

Since a lot of people confuse the terms Invention, Innovation and Entrepreneurs, I would like to compare and contrast them, at least the way I view them.

Invention is about creating something entirely new. The US Patent office defines an Invention as "a new, useful process, machine, improvement, etc., that did not exist previously and that is recognized as the product of some unique intuition or genius".

An Innovation on the other hand is people putting their ideas into valuable action. This means that any individual or organization is capable of Innovation. Berkley school, of Business defines Innovation as 'People and Organizations creating value by perpetually adapting and developing new processes, ideas and products'.

There are several differences in my mind between Innovations and Inventions.

An Invention can cause an Innovation, but many Inventions are often created and then never used. There are several large Organizations that have developed plenty of patents that never ever get to the general community. Something invented but not put into practical use is NOT an Innovation. Most Inventions are meant to create a significant change to a present condition.

Innovations reflect incremental changes in a product or service, or substantial changes in a market. Inventions can best be described as a creation of something that did not previously exist.

Entrepreneurship on the other hand does not necessarily require Innovation. However Entrepreneurship may involve a particular form

Ask for Forgiveness
Not for Permission

of Innovation to produce a new business or new initiative within an existing business.

So just where do Entrepreneurs fit into the equation? Entrepreneurs exist to dramatically change a market by bettering it. Entrepreneurs want to change the existing and are therefore always leaning towards capitalizing on someone else's Invention.

Some people create Inventions which are never brought to the market for profitable use, and hence they are not valuable nor are they innovative.

An Entrepreneurs' Passion

I was shopping at Sam's Club, a leading membership club and one of the nation's top 10 largest retailers, when I suddenly noticed something on the wall. Curiosity got the better of me and I walked up to see the picture of Sam Walton, founder of Wal-Mart and Sam's Club.

Under the picture were the words that I believe are a masterpiece in their own right and something that I, as an Entrepreneur, will always remember and follow.

The Entrepreneurs Creed

"I do not choose to be a common man. It is my right to be uncommon— if I can. I seek opportunity not security. I do not wish to be kept a citizen humbled and dulled by having the state look after me. I want to take the calculated risk; to dream and to build, to fail and to succeed.

I refuse to barter incentive for a dole; I prefer the challenges of life to the guaranteed existence; the thrill of fulfillment to the stale calm of utopia. I will not trade freedom for beneficence nor my dignity for a handout. I will never cower before any master nor bend to any threat.

It is my heritage to stand erect, proud and unafraid; to think and act for myself, to enjoy the benefit of my creations and to face the world boldly and say "this, with God's help, I have done."

Never get angry in Business...

In other words
Do not let your Tongue
Speak faster
Than your Mind

All this is what it means to be an Entrepreneur".

The author of this masterpiece is unknown, though some believe it was written by Dean Alfange during the cold war, and was originally published in This Week Magazine, and later reprinted in the Readers Digest, October 1952 and January 1954.

The words speak of Opportunity verses Security, Calculated Risk to Dream and to Build, to Fail and to Succeed. It also emphasizes that there will be threats on the road to victory and success will depend on how much you are willing to give in, how much you are willing to bend.

In summation, no matter which category you belong to, it is evident that the *desire to be successful must be balanced with the acceptance of a possible failure*. It must also be acknowledged that we need to know ourselves well before we can hold on to the baton and charge ahead to rule the world of business.

CHAPTER 9

Mistakes and Failures

Winners

Never stop

Learning

Success is Failure turned inside out

It is not easy to fail or to even accept failure. Failure is that virtue that can either make us or break us. It can cause permanent damage to the minds and hearts and the confidence of people. And ask those that have been broken by failure; they are constantly haunted by unpleasant memories of the past. These memories are like shadows that follow them around, no matter where they go.

They feel like an animal in a cage, with no possibility of any exit, physical or emotional. The mind feels so trapped that it cannot entertain possibilities of any exit and therefore of any success. They are so convinced that they just cannot do it; and therefore, they will not even try.

As President Abraham Lincoln has said and I quote "My great concern is not whether you have failed, but whether you are content with your failure."

For those that failure could not break are those that have realized success. Failure to them is a friend who taught them well. It is also a stepping stone to wisdom. These men and women are convinced that true failure only happens when one gives up.

History has been very kind to President Abraham Lincoln. He has been portrayed as probably the greatest President of the United States of America. He has taught the world that it is not only very important not to quit, but to always try and be ahead of the game.

It is a good thing that history has been kind to Entrepreneurs and also recorded his failures. It reflected his frail humanity but also showed his attitude of never giving up.

These failures did not stop him, but instead encouraged him to continue to move forward. The following is a short list of his ups and downs... and ups again.

Failures are only permanent
If we stop trying

The only real failure
Is the failure not to move on

1831—Failed in business
1832—Defeated for legislature
1833—Again failed in business
1834—Elected to legislature
1835—Sweetheart died
1836—Had a nervous breakdown
1838—Defeated for speaker
1840—Defeated for elector
1843—Defeated for Congress
1846—Elected for Congress
1848—Defeated for Congress
1855—Defeated for Senate
1856—Defeated for Vice-President
1858—Defeated for Senate
1860—ELECTED PRESIDENT

He was defeated more times than he won, but that did not mean he was a failure.

A breakthrough may just be a few steps away. What a pity for those of us who would stop moving on. As far as I am concerned, the only way to deal with failure is to learn from it and move on.

The end result for Mr. Lincoln was that he became President and through his influence, was able to defend the constitution by winning the Civil War. He even attempted to give voting rights to the Blacks for which he was assassinated. Though he has been long gone yet he is remembered dearly by all even today. His very name is a legacy of success and an inspiration to Entrepreneurs, young and old.

Entrepreneurship Failures

Entrepreneurial Success requires Entrepreneurial Failure. Entrepreneurship research focuses predominantly on success which ignores the high failure rate of new ventures and precludes a holistic view of the Entrepreneurial process.

Don't hide your Failures
Advertise them

I will always ask three simple questions:

- how do Entrepreneurs experience failure
- how do they cope with it
- what do they learn from it

Seasoned business builders typically shy away from any public acceptance and exposure of their failures, and do not report their own mistakes to the world. As someone who lives in this ever changing world of business, it is refreshing to observe that even the best Entrepreneurs make the very same mistakes I have made; wrong assumptions, missed opportunities, lack of foresight and poor judgment—all necessary lessons on the road to success.

Large venture capital firms have admitted making investment mistakes along the way due to reasons which at the time sounded extremely convincing. They had a chance to invest in some of the most profitable companies in the world and they did not—why—because at the time it seemed like a bad idea.

Google—Sergey and Larry rented a garage from a friend for their first year in business. In 1999 and 2000 this friend tried to introduce these two young individuals to several investment firms with no luck. After all two Stanford students trying to write a search engine did not sound exciting at all—students?... a new search engine? Well... the rest is history!

Federal Express—A professor at the University of Yale turned down undergraduate Fred Smith's paper of starting an overnight mail service. The professor gave him a 'C' and turned the paper back with the remark that the idea would never work. Fred made it work!

eBay—Coins? Baseball cards? Used items for sale? 'You must be kidding', said a senior executive in a large investment Company. The idea worked and is still working... strong!

The list can go on and on and on.

Keep going even when
Things seem impossible
With the hope
That there is always a Way...
You just have to look for it

Personal Losses in Business

My wife Persis and I were invited to dinner at a friend's house where I had the opportunity to speak with an Entrepreneur that had grown and exited a very successful business, and is now retired.

During our conversation he narrated a story that will not only resonate with Entrepreneurs, but will also describe the pains we go through while growing and nurturing a business.

Like most Entrepreneurs, he had a line of credit with a bank that helped him manage the cash flow requirements of the business. One day the banker visited him at his new facility and remarked that the business must be really prospering as the new facility was much bigger and better than the previous one.

To this the Entrepreneur replied, "This new facility is the result of me never having got a chance to see my son grow up and take his first step, or be there at his first day at school, or be at the dinner table when he played with his food or even ride his bike for the first time. This is the result of me not being around to see him stumble and fall, yet get back up and walk again. This is a reminder to me of those times that have gone by, times that I missed that will never ever return".

This person was a smoker, but gave up smoking the day his grandson was born. Asked why, he replied with teary eyes, "I do not want to make the same mistake again. I want to do with my grandson what I never did with my son. I want to live to see him graduate".

And I pray that he does.

These personal losses are inevitable in business and are the price an Entrepreneur pays for being ultimately successful. And there are many such instances like this, not just one.

When fear triumphs...
Greed and emotion
Override reason

What type of Entrepreneur are you?

So what is your DNA like?

1. Are you the type that likes to bring people together and operate in a harmonious environment through mentoring?
2. Do you fall in a class of Entrepreneurs that are fiercely independent and believe that you have the answer to all problems?
3. Will you operate only after you have understood the whole situation and are certain that there will be no abrupt changes?
4. Are you that type that jumps on an impulse and just wants to make it then happen?
5. Are you of the opinion that starting a business from a garage and growing one customer at a time is the way?
6. Would you rather be opportunistic and focus on an industry that will enable you to make money quickly?
7. Do you think that going *public* as soon as possible is the way to success?

Some Entrepreneurs started with lemonade stands or door-to-door selling. Others have collected and traded stamps or baseball cards. Still others have always dreamed about making lots of money in life by getting good grades in school.

I believe that the seeds of Entrepreneurship and Entrepreneurial greatness are sown way early in life through our childhood experiences and of course our DNA. Having to choose between financial security and a satisfying and fulfilling life, is one of the most difficult decisions you will face as an Entrepreneur.

Ask yourself this question. Are you...

- a rule breaker
- a rule bender
- a rule follower

Mentoring Entrepreneur...
Harmony, togetherness,
always wants to be liked

Independent Entrepreneur...
Knows it all and do it all too

Cautious Entrepreneur...
No sudden changes, all well planned

Impulsive Entrepreneur...
Just wants to make it happen

There is no right or wrong answer here. This is a matter of behavior and how much risk you are willing to take in business. A noted psychologist that has studied super-successful Entrepreneurs compares them to *well adjusted juvenile delinquents*.

Being able to find the right opportunity, one that fits with your gifts and passions, and one that enables you to be really successful, is one of the most important skills for any Entrepreneur.

The cliché, 'I learn more from my Failures than my Successes' applies directly to Entrepreneurship and growing Organizations.

Although it is difficult to go back in time and reflect upon your mistakes, I personally do that quite often. I do it simply to study my own failures, understand what I did wrong and what I could have done differently, learn as much as I can from my mistakes and move on.

So my dear Entrepreneur….how will you master your end result? You certainly do not know everything but you can always evaluate yourself and determine your attitude to failure. You can either allow it to break you or allow it to make you.

Your call entirely!

CHAPTER 10

Entrepreneurism...
The Aga Khan Way

An Entrepreneur can only lead
If there is no
Conflict or Compromise
Between the Qualities of
Leadership
And
Entrepreneurism

Entrepreneurship without the Religion

I have promised myself that as an Author, I will not venture into writing anything remotely connected with either religion or politics, for two reasons; firstly, I am not qualified to write anything about either topic and secondly, my focus is on Entrepreneurship, motivation, leadership, growth and business.

But being an Entrepreneur I am always intrigued by people and cultures that practice Entrepreneurism rather than preach it. I am a firm believer that our world will be a much better place to live in if we have more of us that can teach others how to grow by being enterprising and self sufficient, rather than simply talk about it.

And by citing an example about His Highness, The Aga Khan and the Ismaili culture, I am neither glorifying it nor am I advocating to anyone to support it or be a follower. Nor am I even suggesting a comparison with any other world culture or religion.

My purpose is simply to focus on the Entrepreneurial aspects of the person and the culture, not the religious or the political side.

Through research and many conversations with groups of Ismailis (as the supporters of Aga Khan choose to call themselves), I have come to realize that there is something called undying obedience, indisputable loyalty and unquestionable faith in the Leadership. There is also something else that I have noticed; a burning desire to serve.

But what amazes me is where does all this come from? How does one accept and self impose such a powerful agenda? Does this originate out of sheer belief, is it faith, is it a simple call to follow; a call that has been passed down from father to son, or is it something else?

On December 17, 2009, His Highness The Aga Khan, was presented with the 'Philanthropic Entrepreneur of the Year 2009 Award" by Le Nouvel Economiste, at a ceremony held at the Cour des Comptes, in Paris, France.

Teach your team
To excel together as one

Lead by example

Philanthropic—means charitable, benevolent, humanitarian and good hearted... one that gives unconditionally and encourages others to do the same.

Combining that with the word Entrepreneur means one that has the ability to create a movement, a wave that encourages people to perform to the best of their abilities—to persuade them to give back to society and to humanity, whatever they can; money, time, skill, knowledge.

Having read about the Leadership, I learned that the Aga Khan is particularly interested in the elimination of global poverty, the advancement of women, the promotion of culture, art and architecture and the promotion of pluralistic values in Society.

As the Founder and Chairman of the Aga Khan Development Network (AKDN), one of the largest private development networks in the world, his main aim is to toil towards social, economic and cultural development in Asia and Africa.

And this is not just limited to the Ismaili community, but also extends to the people with whom the Ismailis share their lives, locally and internationally.

What does all this translate into for an Entrepreneur?

Now what does all this mean to an Entrepreneur.

Firstly as a Leader, the Aga Khan has earned everyone's attention and has focused the entire community on one critical aspect; growth through service. Remember my definition of a Leader—one that is a dealer in hope; a catalyst that removes all obstacles so people can operate to their full potential.

And focus on growth is one vital characteristic of an Entrepreneur. If an Entrepreneur does not grow his business, it will die a natural death.

To be a Leader
One has to be interested first
Before being interesting

Secondly, he has created a culture where people want to share their strengths for the betterment and common good of society.

At every call for duty, he ignites the spirit of Entrepreneurism and allows those that respond, to display and use their strengths and their capabilities and contribute to success, and in the process bettering and growing them into something unimaginable.

I know of Ismailis that have given up their jobs, closed down their businesses and moved to wherever duty calls. As one person told me, "The Boss calls and we respond... no questions asked".

But what does all this do for the individual that follows the Leader when called upon to do so.

I believe it is a path that moves him closer to being an Entrepreneur. His potential is expanded to the fullest, as his capabilities are constantly on display. He knows that there are people that are dependent on his performance and that he is constantly being watched. That brings out the very best in a person.

And after their task is complete, they go back to their earlier routine, much wiser, more connected and above all more accomplished. They can now use what they learned to better their own businesses and thereby their own lives and the lives of people dependant on them.

As one Ismaili gentleman that had just returned from his call for duty told me, "We are charged up spiritually, mentally, emotionally and also physically. The quest to serve is foremost in our minds and nothing else really matters at the time. It is an honor and a privilege to be selected to serve".

There are many people today that have the capability but do not have the opportunity. They have the skills but no avenue to perform. They possess the knowhow but lack the chance to succeed. They have the passion but do not know how to get started.

The Best way to lead a team
In the Future
Is to Connect with them
In the Present

Knowledge and resource sharing through partnerships, encourages individuals to align themselves for a common cause. In the process they are encouraged to perform to the best of their abilities and to discover through self evaluation, new opportunities that they had never even thought of before.

The Aga Khan has played an instrumental role in reaching out to segments of society by enabling individuals to strengthen their Entrepreneurial base and skills, and build financial, social and emotional capital for a sound and secure future.

But the Aga Khan also demonstrates a human side to his success by admitting that all has not worked as planned.

When accepting the 'Philanthropic Entrepreneur of the Year 2009 Award", he said that "... the major principles guiding the AKDN are difficult to implement, and we are met with occasional disappointment. But we have had enough successful achievements, however, to convince us to stay the course".

This to me is the Entrepreneur in him admitting that the path ahead is slippery, but convinced and determined enough to stay the course.

It tells me that no matter how big you are, it is important to accept challenges and admit disappointment, but forge ahead knowing that the best is yet to come.

We need to be the change that we are looking for in this world. We need to accept that there are obstacles in life that will cause a temporary *glitch* in our plans, but those obstacles will not cause us to stop permanently. They are meant to enable us to pause, rejuvenate and then continue on again, on the road to success.

It is the belief that troubles will not last forever. It is the faith that lies within, that will keep us going from strength to strength. It is the acceptance that service above self ultimately strengthens us from the inside and prepares us for our next assignment in life.

That to his Highness, I believe, is Entrepreneurism ... The Aga Khan Way!

CHAPTER 11

My Conclusion

Nature has given us
Two ends...

One to sit on
And one to think

Our Success or Failure
Is dependent

One the One we use most

Make it Happen

It is small moments, experiences through failure, and quiet victories that have made my journey worthwhile.

Someone once asked me, "Why do you always insist on taking the hard road". And I replied, "Why do you assume I see two roads"?

Most people measure success by the amount of power they have or the quantum of money they possess. My rule for measurement of success is quite different.

> ***Success to me is not walking like a king.***
> ***It is walking like you do not care***
> ***who the king is!***

And that only happens when you do not chase your dreams but live your dreams.

I have seen people grow from ground-level positions to being very successful business people. And they all achieved greatness and success because they all believed that they could do it. They all believed in themselves, every one of them.

Life's experiences have enlightened me to accept the fact that sometime during the course of our business lives, each and every one of us needs a mentor, a guide, a coach to help us get through those uncertain times in our lives.

A mentor is a wise and trusted counselor. A mentor is someone that allows you to see the hope inside yourself. Mentoring is a brain to pick, an ear to listen, and a push in the right direction.

A mentor does not necessarily have to be a very successful individual, though it would help to be enlightened by his failures.

Quit thinking about
Thinking to quit

He just needs to hold you accountable for all that you do or are contemplating of doing. A mentor cannot act as your friend but instead needs to counsel you and hold you responsible for your thoughts and actions.

My Entrepreneurial journey has made me realize the importance of my life partner's involvement in my business ventures.

It has made me wiser and trained me to accept the fact that people are different; they think differently, act differently and are motivated differently too. And therefore they must be dealt with differently as well.

Life has taught me that you inherit your family, but you must develop the good sense to choose your friends and business partners wisely. Friends are not those that have been by your side the longest, but those that came in your time of need and never left your side.

I have learned that it not only takes courage to venture down the path of success; one needs to have faith, patience, perseverance and most importantly the burning desire to succeed. There is no such thing as a short cut in business. We need to keep moving but must learn also to stay the course.

Experiences have taught me that you are a student all your life, and the faster you accept this fact, the easier it will get as you sail along you road to success.

Let us all learn from our children for they are the best Entrepreneurs in life. They have demonstrated time and again that they are not afraid to venture out and try new things.

And of course they have never had, nor will they ever have fear of the word NO; a classic ingredient in the pot of success. Our children need more 'role' models and less 'rule' models.

The 'ABC' of Success

Attitude...
Inner Motives and Desires

Behavior...
Actions and Plans

Consequences...
Outcomes and Rewards

On the other hand, I have also come in contact with many people that have never ever had a break in life. They are educated, smart, intelligent and even motivated, but have always missed the boat altogether.

Now how can we explain that? What do we call that—destiny?

No opportunities, no successes in-spite of trying very hard, and the sense of constant failure have moved these individuals from thinking 'faith' to 'fate'.

Life, through Entrepreneurism, has taught me so many little things that it is indistinctively hard not to list at-least a few of them. These lessons that I learned, serve as a reminder of the times that I thought I knew it all, but was dead wrong!

Here are a few of my favorites, in no particular order, that have helped me navigate through my voyage in life and business...

- S.I.E.E. syndrome (SAVE much, INCOME increase, EXPENSE reduction, EDUCATION certainly helps, EXPERIENCE is the glue to financial stability)
- I learned that you derive strength from a close family and even closer friends
- Prepare your team for adversity
- A successful businessman must have the stability and ability to predict
- Success is that old ABC—Ability, Breaks, Courage
- Adapt yourself and learn to work under uncertainty
- Always deliver superior performance
- Make quality the predominant task of every person in your organization
- I learned that hard work always pays in the end but smart work helps you get there faster
- A majority vote does not always determine what is right and what is wrong

Mistakes should not
Be punished

They should be used as
A lesson
For Future success

- He that has the gold, makes the rule
- As Samuel Johnson has said, "Clear your mind of the word—can't"
- We always have choices in life. We can grumble all we want about 'targets' or we can do what it takes to meet them
- Borrow as little as possible
- Spend only after you have earned it
- The Lord did not do it in one day so what makes me think I can

To Sum it all up

I remember what our 14 year old son Kyrus, once told me years ago, when we were walking on a rope-bridge during one of our family vacations.

The bridge was shaking side-to-side and the fatherly instinct in me immediately turned to him and said "Hold my hand son, there is a chance that you may fall".

And to my utter surprise he looked at me and answered "No dad, you hold my hand please. Out of complete fear I may leave your hand, but I know that no matter what, you will never leave mine".

If after reading this book about my Entrepreneurial journey, should you come to realize that you need to hold my hand, I will certainly be there.

For when I travelled through my Entrepreneurial journey, I did not have many people that I could turn to, in my time of need, to hold mine.

So dear Entrepreneur....

Do you really have the GUTS
To GAIN your GLORY

If the answer is YES, then get started. The time to start is not tomorrow or in the future. It is NOW!

What matters is not
How hard you can hit...

It is how hard a hit you can take

Do not let failed attempts deter your ambitions or scare you to take the next step, for you must learn how to overcome failure.

Remember, Failure is simply the Opportunity to begin again, this time more intelligently.

I wish you success in your journey and sincerely hope that may your right hand always be stretched out in friendship, never in want.

And finally, remember, everything that has happened to you is either an opportunity to grow or an obstacle to keep you from growing.

You get to choose!

Believe in Yourself

If you feel responsible
For your past...
It should only be
So that you may learn
From your mistakes

Winning simply means
That you are now better than
You were before

If you want to follow your dream...
Wake up

Successful people are those
That do what needs to be done,
When it needs to be done

Planning...
Determine where you want to go

Organizing...
Facilitate the pursuing of planned goals

Staffing...
Leverage resources—human and financial

Leading...
Create an environment for success

Controlling...
Confirm and track planned path

Life is not fair...
Get used to it

If you are not big enough
To lose
You are not big enough
To win

A ship is always safe in a harbor;
But that is not what a ship is built for

Go with your Intuition

Be very persistent

Stay the course

Stay humble

Think like a wise man
But communicate
In the language
Of the people

Education is what you get from reading
the small print;
Experience is what you get
from not reading it

Listen Carefully... when a
Silent Partner Speaks

Do not Hesitate...
For he who Hesitates
Is lost

To be successful
One needs to
Seek opportunity
Not security

The Impossible
Is often
The untried

The Thing that we call Failure
Is not the Falling down
But the Staying down

Quality is Seen
Service is Felt

ABOUT THE AUTHOR

Nozer Buchia, also referred to as *"Mr. Motivator"*, is an internationally acclaimed motivational, inspirational and keynote speaker of repute. He is known as a *speaker's-speaker* due to his dynamic inimitable style of humor and delivery, and his practical approach to any situation.

His straight-from-the heart, high energy and passionate message has motivated audiences worldwide, and has enabled them get out of their comfort zone and get into greatness.

Nozer Recently received the 2013 DISTINGUSHED ENTREPRENEUR AWARD from the Leadership Academy at the Carol Vance Prison Unit located in Sugar land, Texas, U.S.A., for his selfless work in the preparation and rehabilitation of prisoners as they are being prepared for release from the prison system. Nozer visits the Prison atleast twice a month and works with the prisoners in helping, guiding and preparing them for the 'real world'. His message of 'Hope' and 'Perseverance' has earned Nozer the moniker of "Mr. Motivator", for he truly changes your thinking and motivates you to ultimately get out of your comfort zone and get into greatness. His message to the world, "Believe in Yourself".

A leader at heart, Nozer is a story teller and a great one at that too. His real life experiences and humorous examples and episodes, are the embodiment of his talks. His message is delivered with great passion and complete conviction, as he has lived what he talks about. His determination, persistence and his never-give-up attitude has enabled him to be successful in life and in the world of business.

"We are all born to win", he says, "but are conditioned to fail... believe in yourself".

His **power of positive thinking,** coupled with his message of **success through failures,** will compel you to look at yourself differently but confidently, and will lead you into empowering yourself and believing in your true worth.

The way he does this is by sharing with his audiences, stories of his own successes and failures, and what he did differently to finally get there. He candidly shares his experiences about mistakes and accomplishments, and how one needs to navigate through life in order to be successful. He also cites examples of triumphant entrepreneurs and what they did in their own lives to achieve success.

Corporations worldwide have benefitted from his motivational and keynote addresses as he helps formulate and communicate corporate strategy with clarity and effectiveness.

He has been a visiting Professor at several Colleges and Universities in India and the USA. Nozer has a background in Computer Programming, Design and Management, a Certificate in 'Organization and Methods Study' and two Bachelor's Degrees in Business Administration. He has done his Business Management from The Australian Institute of Management and has earned an MBA in Strategic Management from Michigan, USA.

Nozer's credentials match his reputation. As a consultant, he has repositioned Organizations in several continents and has assisted several individuals and Corporations worldwide in recognizing their true potential and value.

Nozer serves on Advisory Boards of Corporations that seek to gain from his advice and counsel. He has also served as a Mentor on the University of Houston's, Bauer College of Business' Mentorship Program.

Nozer was born in Mumbai (Bombay), India. His daughter Shiraz and his son Aarish live with their families in Sydney, Australia, while he now lives in Houston, Texas, USA, with his wife Persis and their son Kyrus.